The Bournonville Ballets

Marie Cathrine Werning (von Kohl) as a naiad in *Napoli*, c.1844. Laterally reversed hand-coloured daguerrotype by Mads Alstrup (?), here reproduced as true (see no.151). The daguerrotype was donated to the Theatre Museum in Copenhagen in 1934 by the heirs of the dancer Johanne Petersen (1844–1934), who was an illegitimate daughter of Marie Werning (von Kohl) and herself a prominent dancer of the Royal Danish Ballet in the 1860s and '70s.

THE BOURNONVILLE BALLETS

A photographic record
1844-1933

Compiled and annotated by
KNUD ARNE JÜRGENSEN

DANCE BOOKS
CECIL COURT LONDON

The author and publishers wish to express their gratitude to the following foundations who have contributed towards the publication costs of this book:

Kong Christian Den Tiendes Fond
Gangstedfonden
SDS Sparekassens Foundation
Otto Mønsteds Foundation
Landsdommer V. Gieses Legat
Carlsbergs Mindelegat for Brygger J. C. Jacobsen
Magasin du Nord Foundation

First published in 1987 by Dance Books Ltd,
9 Cecil Court, London WC2N 4EZ

British Library Cataloguing in Publication Data
The Bournonville ballets: a photographic
   record 1844–1933.
   1.   Bournonville, August——Performances
   2.   Ballet——Denmark——History
   I.   Jürgensen, Knud Arne
   792.8'45   GV1667

   ISBN 0-903102-98-6

Filmset and printed in Great Britain by
BAS Printers Limited, Over Wallop, Hampshire

For
NINI

Contents

DIVERTISSEMENTS

OPERAS

Foreword

This book is a tribute to a partnership that we nowadays tend to take for granted – that of the dancer and the photographer. Photography came to the service of ballet very early in its development and, as its technology progressed, grew to become an indispensable medium of record. With any invention there must be regret that it did not come sooner, and in the case of photography one might sigh at the thought that it did not preserve the rich flowering of Romantic ballet, although on reflection we might be thankful that the glorious lithographs that form the main pictorial record of that period stand unchallenged. For in its infancy photography was an awkward process that required cumbersome equipment and long exposure times, and the earliest photographs of dancers give no indication of their artistry and have little more than archival significance.

The earliest process by which dancers were photographed was the daguerreotype, a method that produced only a single picture from each exposure. Fanny Elssler had her portrait taken by this process in Philadelphia in 1841, and although the daguerreotype is lost, it has been preserved in a carefully copied lithograph. In the following year Antoine Claudet lured to his London studio several dancers who were then appearing at Her Majesty's Theatre, including the ballerina in vogue, Fanny Cerrito, but these daguerreotypes too seem to have disappeared. A later daguerreotype of Fanny Elssler in costume exists in Hamburg, and there may well be portraits of other dancers awaiting discovery.

With the invention of the collodion process, followed shortly by the exploitation of the carte-de-visite format, multiple copies could be made and photography came within reach of the general population. Photographs of celebrities were offered for sale, and people of quite modest means began to have their portraits taken. The theatre was quick to make use of this new invention and – to give one example – from 1858 until 1864 the Paris Opéra commissioned the photographer Disdéri to record in carte-de-visite format the entire casts of its ballet and opera productions. Later, improved technology brought better quality, and with the exposure time reduced, something of the dancer's style began to be caught. In the twentieth century further developments led to the action photograph and cinematography.

This book is concerned with the ballet at the Royal Theatre in Copenhagen, which ranked as a centre of secondary importance in the nineteenth century but today, in retrospect, is recognised as a prime source of knowledge about the Romantic ballet. For August Bournonville, who directed the ballet there, with two brief intervals, from 1830 to 1877, created a vast repertoire of ballets, a number of which have miraculously survived, thanks to the devotion of successive ballet-masters to preserving what they realised was an important legacy. From the earliest days of photography, dancers have been portrayed in his ballets, and in this extraordinary assemblage, the Danish ballet historian and musicologist, Knud Arne Jürgensen, lifts the curtain of the past and enables us to catch a glimpse, often scene by scene, of these works, some of them we can still see in performance today, although, as the photographs show, the style of production has naturally varied. Taken together, these photographs give us not only an insight into the creative genius of a great choreographer, but an understanding of how ballet appeared to the spectator a century ago.

IVOR GUEST

ix

Acknowledgements

Having worked exclusively on this book for an entire year, I find, at its conclusion, numerous debts of gratitude to be repaid.

First of all, this album would never have come into existence were it not for its publisher, David Leonard of Dance Books Ltd. On a visit to London in January 1985 I had occasion to meet with Mr Leonard for a discussion on another future book project. At the end of this pleasant meeting he remarked that a more *visual* approach to the Bournonville tradition in book form had, according to his view, long been missing in the otherwise large body of Bournonville literature published in recent years. He therefore suggested that an album of the complete Danish Romantic ballet prints should be done with complete annotations and a full account of the dancers and style depicted, such as had recently been published by Dance Books in Edwin Binney's marvellous *Glories of the Romantic Ballet* (1985).

At first I was a little reluctant to accept the commission for such a project, feeling that, though considerable in numbers, the Danish ballet prints have in recent years been rather over-reproduced in the vast literature that followed the 1979 centenary of August Bournonville's death. While explaining these reservations of mine, the discussion naturally turned toward the body of historic Bournonville ballet photography. With his open-minded attitude to this important share of the Bournonville ballet heritage, the content and arrangement of such a Bournonville album was soon defined and commissioned, and the work could be started.

Half-way through, Mr Leonard visited me in Copenhagen for a follow-up discussion on the final arrangement and format of the book, and only four months later the manuscript was ready. I have felt the need for this account of what I see as an exemplary and fruitful co-operation between writer and publisher, and without which this album would never have achieved its present comprehensive character.

Other debts to be repaid are, of course, for the valuable suggestions and practical assistance I have received from the libraries and photographic collections I have approached during the research and collecting of the 478 photographs in this book. Three collections are here of major importance:
a) The Picture Department of Copenhagen's Royal Library, where former and present curators, Mr Bjørn Ochsner and Mr Ib Rønne Kejlbo, have been most co-operative, and Mr Hans Berggreen, who has assisted me patiently in going through the vast number of ballet photographs to be found in that collection.
b) The Theatre Museum in the old Court Theatre at Copenhagen's Christiansborg Palace, where the curator, Mrs Lisbet Grandjean, and her staff trusted me to go through the impressive but still partially uncatalogued collection of ballet photographs preserved in this splendid museum.
c) The Archive of Copenhagen's Royal Theatre, whose curator, Mrs Marianne Hallar, and librarian, Mrs Ida Poulsen, have marvellously assisted me in my continual enquiries, of which the most significant result is the forty-five stage pictures I have included here (see Introduction – Décor).

A number of private collectors have been consulted, of whom I am especially grateful to Mrs Elly Beck, the daughter-in-law of ballet-master Hans Beck; Mr Erik Merrild, son of dancer Karl Merrild; Mrs Ellen Freddie, 'grandchild' of dancer Ellen Price de Plane; Mrs Maja Castenskiold, daughter of dancer Ellen Tegner; and Mr Tucke Tuxen, great-great-grandchild of August Bournonville.

A special thanks is to be given Patricia N. McAndrew for allowing me to quote from her excellent translation of the complete Bournonville scenarios as published in *Dance Chronicle* (1979–83), here employed in the captions.

My gratitude is also due to my fellow dance scholars Mr Erik Aschengreen and Mr Allan Fridericia, whose interest in and suggestions for this work have been a constant encouragement to me.

Finally, I feel deeply obliged to record my gratitude to the photographers, those who originally took the 478 photographs between 1844 and 1933 as well as the four photographers who provided me with the reproduction copies needed for this album, namely Mr Børge Tranberg and Mr Erik Jul Christensen from the Royal Library's photographic studio, Mr Bent Man Nielsen of The Arnamagnian Institute (University of Copenhagen), and Mr Niels Elswing, The National Museum, Copenhagen.

Last, but very far from least, my appreciation and gratitude should be expressed to the curator, Mrs Eva-Brit Fanger, and my colleagues in the Music Department of the Royal Library, who have all shown genuine interest in this project and continually encouraged me in its completion – feeling, like me, the importance of presenting to the dance world of today this illuminating part of the Bournonville heritage.

Copenhagen,   KNUD ARNE JÜRGENSEN
June 1986

x

Introduction

While in the concluding phase of writing this book, I have come to ask myself on a number of occasions, what would have been the comments of August Bournonville, had he been presented with this album, depicting both his now long-lost ballets and those still in repertory, but here captured and exposed for posterity through photographs alone.

I believe that he, at first sight, would have been pleasantly surprised to see the great number of his ballets which had actually survived him for so many years – even finding eight full-length ballets plus six minor divertissements and single dances being extensively performed in Denmark, and worldwide.

Moreover, I can imagine Bournonville as particularly satisfied to know that a photographic album of this kind, focusing exclusively on a single nineteenth-century choreographer, could probably only have been done to such extent in Denmark, and on him, owing to the astonishing, continuous performance tradition of his ballets, which, as an immediate by-product, provided us with a vast and unique photographic documentation.

Finally, I can imagine that Bournonville, had he lived today, would have moderated his otherwise strong antipathy to ballet photography, knowing that it is due to his ballets and their long performance tradition that Denmark should be regarded as being in the absolute front-line when it comes to the photographic documentation of nineteenth-century European ballet.

In its first primitive decades the photographic art was certainly not to Bournonville's liking. With the invention in 1839 of the daguerreotype by French stage designer Louis-Jacques-Mandé Daguerre, this new medium was still for many years considered a rather mysterious if not actually diabolic appendix to the art of painting. In this early period of photography, European ballet was in the midst of an extraordinarily flourishing period, unlike anything to be found in the previous or following centuries. The great popularity of dance in the 1840s and '50s thus caused a number of the leading ballerinas of the Romantic Ballet to 'be taken' by this new astonishing medium, in spite of the considerable costs involved during the first two decades of photography. The price in Denmark for a daguerreotype taken by the domestic Mads Alstrup (see note for no. 151) in 1842 was five Rix-dollars – that is, converted to the purchasing power of today in the UK and USA about £29 sterling or $36.

This fact may explain, in part, why the otherwise highly photogenic art of ballet was not more extensively photographed in Denmark during this early period of photography. Added to this should also be the outspoken aversion of Bournonville to photography, which could explain why so few Danish dancers were tempted to have their portraits made by this new medium. In the first volume of his memoirs *My Theatre Life* (1848) Bournonville published a 15-verse poem on the daguerreotype phenomenon, in which he a little rigidly states:

(v. 1) The daguerreotype's grinning portrait
        I'll not hesitate to set
        In a class with an automaton – or a marionette.

(v. 2) It may do for architecture:
        A building's cold lines to immure;
        But ne'er can it hope to rival the glories of Nature.

(v. 4) *Chimie* itself, aided by *méchanique*,
        May only be said to approach *plastique*
        To the same degree that a hurdy-gurdy can ever be called *musique*.

(v. 6) People loudly exclaim: 'But can't you see
        That this picture truly resembles me?
        Why it bears the stamp of *Reality*.

(v. 7) But truth without spirit is really Death,
        And, loveless, he steadily wandereth,
        Seeking to rob each thing of its breath.

(v. 10) For the graveyard's silence and peace of mind
        In a lifelike picture are two of a kind;
        For the soul in a death-mask you'll never find.

(*Translation by Patricia McAndrew*)

For a dance researcher preparing a photographic album of the Bournonville ballets, this reading should, of course, look rather discouraging at first sight. However, with the continuous development of the photographic art that took place after the 1860s and throughout the following seven decades, I feel that even Bournonville would have appreciated the value of getting together within the systematised scope of an album the vast number of photographs of his ballets taken in this period.

My main motive in presenting this important share of Bournonville heritage to today's dance world derived from the surprising discovery of the great number of photographs actually taken during the ninety years performance period between 1844 and 1933. From these years I have traced almost six hundred photographs for a total of twenty-four ballets, five divertissements, and four opera divertissements, of which only about 120 have previously been published. This fact convinced me of the necessity of presenting a reasonable amount of this Bournonville legacy to the audience, for whom the Bournonville ballets have long since become a precious possession.

By selecting and annotating 478 photographs from this splendid material, I hope to have rendered possible a clarification of some of the built-in information to be found in these photographs. Should I thereby succeed in spurring my fellow dance scholars to further studies in the development of the Bournonville tradition, as well as providing future producers of the Bournonville ballets and today's audiences with a better and deeper understanding of the lasting qualities that lie within Bournonville's ballets, I believe the objectives of the book will have been accomplished.

To put a reasonable limitation on this album I chose at an early stage the year of 1933 as the last to be covered, in this way setting up a sort of line of demarcation to what could be called 'the era of the old Bournonville style' as opposed to that known in our time. With Harald Lander's appointment as ballet-master of the Royal Danish Ballet in 1930, the works of the Bournonville repertory achieved, thanks to Lander's thorough revisions, their definitive forms, which have remained the basis for all later productions to this day within the Royal Danish Ballet.

By presenting only the photographs for the Bournonville ballets as they appeared up to 1933, I hope to have put together a collection which could serve as an illuminating counterpart to the Bournonville repertory known from today's performances, thereby making it possible for today's audiences better to understand what is actually meant by 'the old style' with regard to costumes, décors, choreographic style and mimic expressiveness. What, then, are the most significant characteristics of this 'old' style?

For the observant eye, the photographic sources presented here can provide if not all then certainly some of the most important answers to that question. Studying closely the characteristics of Bournonville's ballets as they appear in this album, it becomes evident that the various elements which constitute a ballet style obviously do not only relate to the aspect of 'how to move'. Equally important here are the stylistic peculiarities of costumes, décors, the dancers' placement of their bodies when in fixed positions, and the degree of body language which constitutes the mimic expressiveness that seems so particular in Bournonville's ballets. These important historic aspects of the 'old' Bournonville style are thus for the first time fully illustrated within this album.

A few introductory guidelines to the most important characteristics of this 'old' style should be given the reader in order to fully read the most informative of the photographs' many inner messages.

COSTUMES

What strikes one at first when going through the photographic sources to Bournonville's ballets is the astonishing diversity of ballet costumes during the ninety continuous years of unbroken performance tradition. Sometimes the costumes for a particular rôle changed completely in both style and outfit from just one decade to another, while others were kept nearly intact for periods of fifty years or more.

A striking example of the first kind is the development between 1866 and 1902 of the costume of Astrid in the 1835 ballet *Waldemar* (nos. 28–33, 41–43, 46). Strong influences from the dominating fashion of the time can clearly be traced here, such as for instance the attached lace trimmings (no. 30), which became almost obligatory to the ballet costume of the 1880s, or the tendency, toward the beginning of our century, in designing dance costumes of more operatic than balletic nature (cf. nos. 42 and 41).

A reason for this often very strong affinity between ballet and opera costumes may well have been the very prosaic one of economy. To economise, many dance costumes were directly adapted from the contemporary opera repertory, or vice versa, a practice which was followed throughout the period covered here, and of which no. 380, depicting a scene from Act III of *The Valkyrie*, is a fine example, with costumes here being partly adapted from Richard Wagner's *Die Walküre*.

However, the extensive adaptation of older costumes also took place from one ballet to another: examples of this can be found in nos. 24, 264, and 438, with Arnold Walbom's costume in *Waldemar* (no. 24) being re-used by Hoppensach in *A Folk Tale* (no. 264), and Waldemar Price's *Waldemar* costume (no. 24) re-used by himself in *Arcona* (no. 438). Of particular interest in connection with the costumes is the footwear, reaching from light dance shoes to the most heavy boots imaginable. On a number of occasions one has cause to reflect on how this striking diversity in footwear, often within a single ballet, must have influenced the dancers' way of moving, be it in dance rôles or mime parts. Examples of this variety can be studied in nos. 18, 34–38, 55, 62, 70, 71, 82, 174, 240, 364, 368, 391, 399, 440, to name only a few.

DECOR

After 1900 the stage director of Copenhagen's Royal Theatre began to have photographs made of the complete sceneries to operas, dramas, and ballets, a tradition which is still maintained at this theatre. The photographs, perhaps taken by the stage director himself, were shot from the first circle in the theatre and served to illustrate in all details how the scenery was composed, being a supplement to the stage director's written records.

From 1900 to 1926 these photos were pasted into the so-called *Maskinmesterprotokoller* (stage director's records), and ever since have been carefully preserved in the Royal Theatre archive. They provide us today with a rare opportunity for a close study of the Bournonville décor through forty-five stage pictures covering a total of fifteen ballets plus three divertissements in operas as staged between 1900 and 1933. When it is taken into consideration that a considerable number of these early stage photos actually depict sceneries which had been kept almost unchanged since Bournonville's own time, the importance of the photos becomes evident.

When Copenhagen's old Royal Theatre was demolished in 1873 to give place to the present theatre building, inaugurated on October 15, 1874 (in the notes referred to as 'the new theatre'), most of the original sceneries for Bournonville's ballets had to be replaced by new sets or adapted from older décors to fit in with the larger dimensions of the new stage. However, these new décors were still in great part made from the older productions, with the exception of only two ballets, *A Folk Tale* (1874 and 1894 productions), and *Waldemar* (1877 and 1894 stagings), which were given what could be called completely new sets.

Because most of the ballets were presented with such very mixed settings from 1874 to 1933 we have today scope for a fascinating study not only of the development of Bournonville's existing ballets, but also of a number of his long lost works, together with some of the contemporary operas and dramas, from which the origin of many sets can be traced (see e.g. photographs and notes for nos. 25, 106, 137, 198, 206, 302, 390, 397, 464).

Moreover, we are given a rare chance to compare the photographs with the scene painters' original sketches that are still preserved in the Royal Theatre archive and the Theatre Museum in Copenhagen. A juxtaposition of these original sketches with the photographs of the sets as they actually looked can thus help us to imagine what the décors of those Bournonville ballets for which no photos exist, but are depicted only through the scene painters' sketches, might have looked like.

The sceneries presented here are all the oldest existing photographs I have been able to trace. In some cases they testify to the little attention that was paid to correctness of style in the first two decades of our century. A number of sceneries have been composed from the strangest mixture of older sets imaginable – here again for economic reasons. This had for many years been a widespread practice at Copenhagen's Royal Theatre, and also happened in Bournonville's own time. However, by 1900 a peak was reached in this extensive re-use of older sets and props without proper attention to the time and style depicted. An outstanding example of this can be seen in no. 206, which, according to Bournonville's original programme, is supposed to depict a magnificent garden in Flanders at the end of the seventeenth century. Here we see a set made up of a Louis XVI-style garden (earlier used in Mozart's *The Marriage of Figaro*) to which are added a number of garden chairs from the 1849 French vaudeville-ballet *Conservatoriet* (see no. 176), and, at centre stage, a Danish renaissance-style dining-room suite borrowed from *A Folk Tale* (see nos. 250, 271). In all a total confusion of styles, again because of economic reasons. Still, a number of the most successful sceneries were kept carefully intact throughout the entire post-Bournonville period, such as the sceneries shown on nos. 61, 137, 148, 155, 176, 213, 224, 315, 390, 397, 424, all testifying to the strong veneration for a scenic continuity in Bournonville's ballets, another important characteristic of the Bournonville tradition.

To help the reader with a general view of the development and changes of the Bournonville sceneries prior to those reproduced here, I have added to the notes in the List of Pictures (see p. 163) the total number of productions of each ballet for which changes were made in the décor. This survey indicates the year of each production as well as giving the names of the scene painters who changed, adapted, or added to the original décors after the ballet's creation and up to 1933.

CHOREOGRAPHIC STYLE

Although the art of photography by its very nature can only capture the dancer's figure and reflect moments, from which the elements that constitute a specific choreographic style can be gleaned, a surprisingly high number of the historic photographs collected here can fully illuminate the most significant stylistic elements of the 'old' Bournonville style. Because most of the pictures presented here were taken with dancers posing rather than actually moving at the moment of shooting, insights into the choreographic style to be obtained from this album will, of course, mainly relate to the dancer's placement of the body, head, arms, and fingers – in other words the delicate interplay of the body's movements which constitute the classic so-called 'Bournonville-*épaulement*'. Outstanding examples of this, all deserving particular attention, are nos. 32, 64, 66, 80, 82, 93, 134–6, 151, 158, 162–3, 173, 196, 240, 242–3, 248, 257, 279, 285–7, 289–90, 300–9, 399, 433, 435, 455–6, 460–2, 473–6.

Focusing on a few of the photographs, those which depict groupings and postures from ballets that are still in repertory should be considered as the most informative when it comes to differences in choreographic style of older times and today. The grouping from *La Sylphide*, Act II (no. 93), and the final Act III grouping of *Napoli* (no. 173) both clearly testify to the many significant changes that have taken place since the end of the last century and up to our time, with regard to grouping, style, and the overall scenic appearance of larger ensemble scenes.

Among the above-listed examples a personal favourite of mine is the 1909 grouping from *Napoli*'s *Pas de six*, shown in no. 158. Pefectly demonstrated by Richard Jensen and Grethe Ditlevsen, this photograph represents a classic example of the sophisticated interplay of soft, naturally curved lines between the two sexes, which is the quintessence of Bournonville's delicate art of posture. Originally a sculpturally inspired choreographic art of posing, this special talent of Bournonville's for choreographing groups of dazzling beauty was later fully developed, and reached a peak in ballets like the Greek mythological *Psyche* (1850) and the Persian 'Arabian Nights' ballet *Abdallah* (1855).

MIME

When studying the photographs in closer detail one soon becomes aware of the many built-in depictions of the dramatic action to be found in most pictures. This fact is even more remarkable when one considers that this is true not only of pictures from the last decades included in this collection, but also applies to a considerable number of the earlier more primitive shots. I have personally been amazed to discover how many of these early photographs can be said deliberately to depict dramatic situations that are fully recognisable when compared with the ballet's libretto, thus clearly aiming to be more than mere dancers' portraits or posed costume pictures.

I therefore believe it reasonable to assume that the many dramatic situations depicted here are, in most cases, those which the artists themselves regarded as the most characteristic and photogenic moments of their interpretations. An outstanding example of this kind is the impressive 1861 series of thirteen photos with dancer Petrine Fredstrup (nos. 3, 14, 122, 132, 175, 189, 208, 227, 251, 273, 294, 311, 457), showing her in all her most prominent rôles. In spite of being taken 125 years ago and almost exclusively showing scenes from now long extinct Bournonville ballets, the dramatic situations represented in this unique series can all be surely identified when compared with the action as described in Bournonville's original libretto. Other examples of this are the two series shot by Peter Elfelt in 1905 and 1911, which depict the complete mime scenes of Act I in *The Wedding Festival in Hardanger* (nos. 214–40). These series are of particular interest here, because it seems as if the photographer has been personally assisted by ballet-master Hans Beck during the shooting of the dramatic highlights in this ballet (see note for no. 214). The mimic expressiveness found in these series is particularly revealing for the insight into that mimic body language, through which Bournonville created what he later called 'the dramatic truth'. The characteristic Bournonville mime, as it appears in these photographs, consisted of free and natural plastic mime-expressions *d'ensemble*, performed with a special mimic *épaulement*, which, at times, may look rather stylised to our eyes today, but nevertheless, in his own time provided the dancers with a language through which they could 'live' within the rôles. This particular *mime d'ensemble*, as seen for instance on nos. 232–3, was expressed from *inside*, that is through beautifully modelled groups, as opposed to the 'outward' conventional dramatic gestures directed at the audience, which have become so predominant in today's performances.

Another striking characteristic of the Bournonville mime is the dancers' carriage, through which all stages of emotions were expressed. Interesting examples of this kind are nos. 262 and 264, both depicting the troll Diderik in *A Folk Tale*. The former, dating from 1903, shows a rather naïve interpretation of this troll figure, while the latter, dating from the ballet's 1854 creation, depicts a more diabolic representation of the same character, thereby revealing how the Bournonville mime, in its origin, was given stronger dramatic and realistic accents, even when it came to such fairy-tale characters as Diderik.

Another fascinating example of this kind is the set of three photographs, depicting the street singer Pascarillo in Act I of *Napoli* (nos. 143–5). Being juxtaposed these photographs show three of the most famous performers in this rôle from its 1842 creation up to 1915. On the earliest (no. 143) we see Frederik Ferdinand Hoppensach giving Pascarillo with a true tragic appearance, dressed in a costume that strongly underlines this character's miserable condition. The Neapolitan street singer or *improvisatore*, as known in the last century, was exactly that same kind of miserable person, who fascinated his contemporaries first of all by his deep wretchedness and sense of tragedy, which he better than anybody could recount, having known the true misery of life in his own right.

According to numerous accounts from visitors to eighteenth- and nineteenth-century Naples, this familiar character was seen more as a tragi-comic human deterrent to his age than as the charming street entertainer he had become by our own century.

In *Napoli* the character of Pascarillo also developed into a much more friendly and harmless mime rôle, as can clearly be glimpsed from Christian Christensen's 1909 parade-like interpretation, dressed in a much more presentable suit with cap and a charmer's scarf (no. 144). A few years later this changing of the rôle toward a more naïve interpretation was even further stressed by Karl Merrild. In his 1915 performance, Pascarillo now appears as a most presentable open-air entertainer, leaving no trace of the character's original tragic-comic misery such as first depicted by Bournonville.

Bournonville's original strong accenting of this so-called 'dramatic truth' was, however, soon considered a little old-fashioned in style, and by the beginning of our century this peculiar mimic expressiveness little by little became reduced to a more conventional-style mime in order to keep up with changing tastes of the audiences. Examples of this can be glimpsed in the depicted mime scenes from *Waldemar* (nos. 39, 42, 46), *The Valkyrie* (no. 364), and *The Lay of Thrym* (no. 406–7), all of which are more operatic than actually balletic in style.

The introduction to an album of this nature would be incomplete without a section on the photographers and the photographic conventions during the ninety years of Danish ballet photography included in this collection.

Besides the more balletic aspects on the development of the Bournonville tradition from the mid-1840s up to 1933, the pictures presented here must also be studied and discussed from the photographic historian's point of view, as important aspects on the development of ballet photography are exemplified, of which a few deserve to be outlined. Seen as a whole, one soon becomes aware of the highly individual approaches to ballet photography as represented by the photographs of the forty-five identified photographers (thirty-five photographic firms) included here.

One of the ways to study and judge the values of these different approaches is to focus on the studio milieu employed, with which the photographers attempt to bring forth the narrative elements of the ballets by using appropriate back-cloths, floor carpets and props. Many interesting examples of this kind can be found, some even representing what must only be called brilliant attempts in recreating the true illusion of theatre environment (e.g. nos. 24, 40, 42, 47, 49, 53–4, 99, 226, 232–3, 313, 423). However, the greatest number of photographs must in this respect be regarded as rather primitive attempts, with studio milieux that in many cases can be claimed as only just acceptable when it comes to the affinity between the studio set and the depicted 'action' of the ballet. In this connection should also be mentioned the sometimes very awkward, if not (unintentionally) comic, photographs that were taken in studios – or outdoors – with back-cloths totally alien to the actual stage setting of the scene depicted, examples of which can be seen on nos. 133, 150, 154, 262, 279, 298, 333, 344, 436, 475, 477.

Another important photo-historic aspect is the photographers' occasional attempts to capture complete dance and mime scenes by means of larger series of photos. Especially important here are the attempts by Georg Lindström and Peter Elfelt, whose series from *La Sylphide* (nos. 62, 67–9, 72–3, 76–81, 84–5, 89, 93, 95, 100–2, 104–5), *The Toreador* (nos. 134–6), *Napoli* (nos. 158–9, 166–7), *The Wedding Festival in Hardanger* (nos. 214–40), and *Far From Denmark* (nos. 318–22, 324–7) are all unique examples in the history of Danish ballet photography of the translation of the transient art of dance into the lasting format of photography.

In these series the photographer's importance as documentarist to ballet history becomes evident, although not all depictions in the series presented here should be regarded as true reflections of what actually took place on stage. A fascinating example of this is the 1903 photograph from *La Sylphide* (no. 67), showing Ellen Price de Plane in the ballet's opening scene as the Sylphide who, carried away with tenderness, approaches the sleeping James and lightly kisses his brow. From this photo we learn that the Sylphide's tenderness for the sleeping James was originally of a much more palpable kind, so to say, compared with what we see performed in the same scene today, when she merely sends a kiss through the air towards the forehead of the slumbering James, having no physical contact with him at all.

However, from the same photograph the observant eye will also discover that the position of Ellen Price de Plane's body and head has deliberately been turned in profile with the photographer's lens, thereby helping Lindström to catch as much of her features as possible within the photograph. This fact probably means that Price de Plane, when performing this scene on stage, was originally turned directly towards James with her back to the audience at the moment of her kissing his brow.

This example, of which many similar can be found in this album, testifies to how carefully these older photos should be 'read' when trying to squeeze out the historic authenticity hidden in them. With examples like this one, the dance historian must often both add to and subtract from the picture at the same time in order to read fully their inner documentary messages, always keeping in mind that the photographs should be regarded first of all as the photographer's individual view of the ballets rather than true reflected images of the Bournonville tradition.

As my aim with this book has been first of all to facilitate a more profound *visual* understanding of the Bournonville heritage for dance scholars and future producers of the Bournonville ballets as well as the public in general, I realised, while in the initial planning phase of this album, that my options for the best communication of this illuminating material were two:

a) to arrange the entire material into a systematised thematic whole with a number of separate sections, each covering those specific aspects of the Bournonville tradition that I have briefly introduced here.

b) to present the photographs of each ballet separately, strictly following the sequence of action, and with the ballets presented in chronological order.

The advantages of both designs were equal, the first being a more thoroughly scholarly approach, while the latter would result in a more accessible progression through Bournonville's productions. However, I definitively chose the second arrangement at the moment when I discovered that the action situations depicted on so many of the 478 photos could be surely identified and given captions by quoting Bournonville's original libretti, which in recent years have all been published in a most scholarly and sensitive English translation by Patricia McAndrew. For those ballets for which no Bournonville libretto exists, I chose to add captions based on his descriptions of the works in his memoirs *My Theatre Life* (also translated by McAndrew: here abbreviated *MTL*), or from his production notes written in the violin scores (the so-called *Répétiteurs*) that were used in rehearsals. For the four operas included (nos. 462–78) captions have been made from corresponding programmes, published in the series *Det kongelige Theaters Repertoire* (Repertory of the Royal Theatre), 1829–76.

By combining the action as described in the original libretti with the dramatic situations shown in the historic photographs, I believe I have fully compensated for not having employed the first, more scholarly, thematic design in this book. To the captions have been added, moreover, the full names of the artists depicted and the characters performed as well as the date (in parenthesis) of the dancer's first performance of the rôle. Finally, each picture has been given a serial number and (in parenthesis) the year for the taking of the photograph; additional, more specific, details and notes can be found under the corresponding number in the book's concluding List of Pictures (p. 163).

The main advantage of juxtaposing the original libretti with the depicted action situations, strictly in order with the work's dramatic development, is that the reader in this way will constantly be reminded of the development, and changes that took place during these ninety years of the Bournonville tradition. By choosing this present arrangement, most ballets will be represented by photographs that, placed side by side, often cover exactly the same situations but can have been taken with intervals of up to seventy-five years, thereby emphasising the continuity of the vast vision of what we today refer to as The Bournonville Tradition.

BALLETS

The Sleepwalker

Ballet in 3 Acts by Jean Aumer.
(*La Somnambule, ou l'Arrivée d'un nouveau seigneur*; Paris Opéra, September 19, 1827).
Music by Ferdinand Hérold with incorporated dances by various composers.
Costumes by Johan Christian Ryge, partly adapted from older repertory (since 1875 by Edvard Lehmann).
Premiered on September 21, 1829, with *mise-en-scène* and choreography by August Bournonville.
Last performance: March 4, 1887.
Number of performances: 126.

With his libretto for *La Somnambule* Eugène Scribe, the admired master of the French comedy, created the dream rôle, so to speak, for the young dramatic ballerinas of the Pre-romantic and Romantic Ballet. The rôle, originally choreographed by Jean Aumer for the French ballerina Pauline Montessù, almost immediately became the touchstone for all dramatic ballerinas of the period.

With the plot's strong emphasis on the inner emotional turmoil of the young Thérèse, who, having sleepwalked into the bedroom of a visiting count (Saint-Rambert), wrongly appears to be betraying her fiancé Edmond, this ballet gave new and strong dramatic impulses to the Pre-romantic French Ballet. The strange mixture of the expressive mimic display of Thérèse's inner turmoil, mingled with a series of daring *scènes piquantes*, secured the ballet's later adaptation by the Romantic Ballet as well, thanks primarily to the plot's focusing on the inner and subconscious conflicts of the human soul.

During his three-year sojourn in Paris, 1826–29, August Bournonville saw *La Somnambule* on a number of occasions and immediately realised that it represented an important step toward the then badly-needed renewal in dramatic ballet writing. He therefore copied the entire score himself and filled it with annotations on both the mime and the dramatic action, such as he had seen during the series of rehearsals he attended prior to the ballet's 1827 premiere at the Paris Opéra. From this score, now one of the most important sources for this ballet, he later staged the entire work with new dances devised by himself during his three-month guest appearance at Copenhagen's Royal Theatre in the autumn of 1829.

The ballet, his first complete mounting of a three-act work, became a tremendous success and was kept in the repertory for the next sixty years. By the late 1880s, however, the plot's rather naïve erotic undertones were no longer as appealing to an audience, now turning more toward the drama of the period, as represented by the more fully developed realism in the plays of Henrik Ibsen. *La Somnambule*'s last restaging by Emil Hansen (October 27, 1886) was thus soon abandoned and the ballet went into oblivion.

The many photographs available for this ballet all but one depict the rôle of Thérèse, and reflect the different emotional stages of her mind, such as her happiness about the imminent marriage with Edmond (nos. 1, 2, 4), her ill-fated sleepwalking in Act II (nos. 5–8), and her utter despair in Act III, when she has been unjustly rejected by her fiancé, who in anger and defiance threatens to marry the jealous innkeeper Gertrude (no. 3), thereby causing Thérèse's breakdown (nos. 9–11). On most of the pictures the photographer has carefully endeavoured to create an actual stage illusion by using appropriate back-cloth and props, thus capturing the highlights of what is perhaps the most demanding mimic rôle in the Romantic Ballet.

1 (1868). Betty Schnell as Thérèse (2.10.1868); Act I:
'. . . In a pas de deux, during which the action progresses, Edmond places his betrothal ring on Thérèse's finger and then gives her a rose . . . Thérèse presses to her lips the rose he has just given her, and hides it in her bosom . . .'

2 (1886). Charlotte Hansen as Thérèse (27.10.1886); Act I:
'. . . Everyone leaves. Edmond and Thérèse also start off, but slowly, and when they find themselves alone, they animatedly rush back to the foreground and display to each other their love, joy and delight. "Now thou art mine, nothing can part us!" . . .'

3 (1861). Petrine Fredstrup as Gertrude (14.10.1848); Act I:
'. . . Madame Gertrude enters and displays her jealousy and animosity [because of Thérèse's and Edmond's forthcoming marriage] "Why are you angry at us" he [Edmond] asks Gertrude. "Must you be our enemy because I will not become your husband?" Gertrude displays her annoyance . . .'

4 (1875). Athalia Flammé as Thérèse (17.12.1875); Act I:
[1874 divertissement]

5 (1886). Charlotte Hansen as Thérèse (27.10.1886); Act II:
'. . . We see Thérèse, clad in simple white garb, her arms and feet bare. Outside the window can be seen the end of the ladder Edmond placed there in Act I; it is by this that Thérèse has climbed up . . .'

6 (1868). Betty Schnell as Thérèse (2.10.1868); Act II:
'. . . She is walking in her sleep and slowly wanders down to centre stage . . .'

7 (1886). Charlotte Hansen as Thérèse (27.10.1886); Act II:
'. . . At this moment she thinks it is the following day, that she hears the bells ringing, that she is in the church with the wedding taking place . . .'

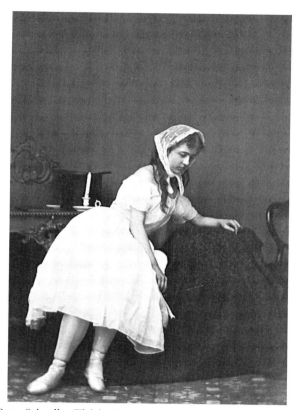

8 (1868). Betty Schnell as Thérèse (2.10.1868); Act II:
'. . . Thérèse has risen from the armchair and draws near the bed. She sits down on it, lays her head in her hand and rests . . .'

9 (1886). Anna Jensen as Thérèse (11.11.1886); Act III:
'. . . [Edmond] grabs Thérèse's hand and removes his betrothal ring. Thérèse [in her wedding dress] is horrified, looks at the hand from which he has taken the ring, and sinks unconscious into the arms of her foster mother . . .'

3

10 (1886). Charlotte Hansen as Thérèse (27.10.1886); Act III:
'. . . She listens and thinks she hears bells ringing for Edmond's wedding . . .'

11 (1886). (cont.) '. . . From her bosom she takes the flower Edmond gave her; it is dry, withered. She waters it with her tears and covers it with kisses . . .'

12 (1868). Betty Schnell as Thérèse (2.10.1868); Act III:
[Wedding dress] '. . . The music begins. At this sudden noise, Thérèse wakens, petrified, dazzled by everything around her, the noise of the instruments, the cries of
joy – all this makes her believe this is a new dream. She holds one hand in front
of her and the other seems to say: "Don't awaken me!" . . .'

4

Faust

Romantic Ballet in 4 Acts.
Music by Philip Ludvig Keck with borrowings from works by Schneitzhoeffer, Carlini, Sor, Spontini, Rossini and Weber.
Costumes by Johan Christian Ryge, partly adapted from older repertory (since 1855 by Edvard Lehmann).
Premiered on April 25, 1832.
Last performance: November 17, 1855.
Number of performances: 53.

Bournonville's *Faust*, his first attempt to stage a ballet taken from classic literature, represents an important step in nineteenth-century European ballet toward a new genre of dramatic ballet writing. Considering that the first volume of the definitive version of Goethe's *Faust* was published in Leipzig in 1808, the second following as late as 1832 (the complete edition was first published in 1838), it becomes evident that in being tempted to stage a three-act *Faust* ballet as early as 1832, Bournonville was extremely well acquainted with the humanistic and literary mainstreams of his time.

His main inspiration for *Faust*, however, may well stem from the Parisian theatre. In 1827 the first lyric attempt to bring this classic to the French stage was realised with Béancourt's opera-drama *Faust*, based on a libretto by Théaulon de Lambert and Gondelier and premiered at the Théâtre de la Nouveauté on October 27, 1827, This important lyric attempt might well have been seen by the young Bournonville, or at least have come to his knowledge, since as early as 1831 (in only his second season as ballet-master in Copenhagen) he had decided to stage a three-act ballet on that same theme. Another contemporary *Faust*, which also must have come to his knowledge, was the opera by Angélique Bertin, premiered at the Théâtre Italien on March 8, 1831. A third, and perhaps the most important, inspiration may have derived from his meeting and friendship with Carlo Blasis during his years of study in Paris, 1826–29. Blasis is known to have sketched a *Faust* sometime between 1825 and 1830, which, however, he did not succeed in staging until many years later in Warsaw (1856) and Moscow (1861).

Bournonville's 1832 *Faust* thus represents the very first attempt on that theme in European ballet history, with the *Faust* ballets by A. Deshayes (London, 1833), S. Taglioni (Naples, 1835), and J. Perrot (Milan, 1848) as the most important followers. Among these *Faust* ballets, Blasis' libretto bears most resemblance to that of Bournonville's, which focuses on the fallen Margaretha and her final salvation through Faust's desperate but heroic agreement with Mephistopheles.

In Copenhagen the ballet had a rather troublesome life on stage, owing most of its weakness to the poor score of Philip Ludvig Keck. Keck, an oboist of the Royal Theatre orchestra, was only capable of delivering light arrangements of fragments pieced together from various contemporary operas and ballets, and seems to have given up halfway in the face of the demanding task of providing a three-act score to Goethe's *Faust*. Although a second, much improved, version was mounted in 1855, the ballet was never really successful and was soon abandoned, to Bournonville's great disappointment. The short life of the ballet explains the very limited number of photographs available for this otherwise most important work.

13 (c. 1849–55). Ludvig Gade as Mephistopheles (8.12.1849); Act I [Faust's Study]: '. . . Thunder crashes, lightning and red flames illuminate the sinister chamber, and out of a bookcase jumps Mephistopheles . . .'

14 (c. 1861). Petrine Fredstrup as Martha (26.9.1845); Act II: '. . .Mephistopheles is exultant [having, with the help of Martha, succeeded in making Margaretha depart for a rendezvous with Faust], and in his wild delight he tries to embrace Martha . . . Martha becomes frightened . . .'

Waldemar

Original Romantic Ballet in 4 Acts.
Music by Johannes Frederik Fröhlich.
Scenery by Arnold Wallich (Acts I & III), Troels Lund (Acts II & IV), and Christian Ferdinand Christensen (Act IV – Grathe Heath).
Costumes by Johan Christian Ryge, partly adapted from older repertory (since 1853 by Edvard Lehmann).
Premiered on October 28, 1835.
Last performance: December 12, 1920.
Number of performances: 233.

Waldemar, Bournonville's first ballet on a Danish national historical theme, was also to become his most successful ever in that genre.

Having staged mainly a number of French ballets during his first seasons as newly appointed ballet-master in Copenhagen, he gained tremendous success with this original ballet, and this encouraged him to work exclusively from his own original libretti in the future. However, the stimulus that first tempted him to create a four-act ballet on the dramatic period in Danish national history when three pretenders to the Danish crown – Svend, Knud, and Waldemar – rivalled each other, came to Bournonville in Paris during the summer of 1834. Here he witnessed the rehearsals at the Théâtre Nautique of the French-Italian choreographer Louis Henry's staging of the four-act ballet-pantomime *Guillaume Tell* (premiered on June 10, 1834, but originally created for San Carlo, Naples, in 1809). Bournonville was deeply impressed by the mastery with which Henry operated large crowds on stage – at that time a distinctive feature of the Italian *mimodrama*, new not only to Bournonville but also to the Parisian stage.

From this theatre experience, as well as from reading various books on Danish national history, Bournonville choreographed an impressive four-act ballet focusing on two of the three pretenders to the Danish crown, the young and brave Waldemar, and the elder, deceitful Svend, whose daughter Astrid falls in love with the handsome Waldemar and helps him to escape from a murderous assault led by her treacherous father during what was meant to be a conciliatory meeting in the castle of Roskilde (Act II).

Among the ballet's many dramatic situations that of the final battle scene in Act IV, when Waldemar raises an army to defeat Svend at Grathe Heath, was of an effectiveness never seen before in Copenhagen. However, the ballet soon underwent a number of drastic revisions not only by Bournonville (1857, 1866, 1872) but also by his successors (Hans Beck, 1893, and Gustav Uhlendorff, 1920), which explain, in part, the remarkable long-lasting success of this otherwise highly passionate patriotic ballet, being constantly adapted to the audience's changing taste over a continuous performance-period of eighty-five years.

This lasting success is clearly reflected by the vast number of photographs available for *Waldemar*. Seen together they serve as an excellent example of the sometimes drastic changes that took place in the performance tradition of the Bournonville classics between 1835 and 1920, with regard to mime (e.g. nos. 20, 23, 24, 27, 34–40) as well as costumes (nos. 28, 30, 31, 33) and décor (nos. 1, 24, 48, 51).

15 (1901). Act I (& Act III): '. . . A clearing in the woods by Issefjord; in the background, Roskilde; to the left, a statue of St. Knud; to the right, the blacksmith's house. Here and there, fishing nets and farming implements. Noon . . .'

16 (1909). Holger Mehnen as a grandchild of Agnar (18.4.1907); Act I: '. . Agnar, who served under Erik Ejegod, is spending his old age with his sons and amuses himself by telling his grandchildren tales of war. The boys, armed with homemade wooden swords, listen attentively to the old man's story . . .'

17 (1901). Ellen Price as Hedvig (7.12.1895) and Gustav Uhlendorff as Erik (8.12.1901); Act I: '. . . Hedvig sights Erik's boat. All jubilantly hasten to the strand. Erik leaps ashore and into his sweetheart's arms . . . he brings a troop of young peasants who are returning from war with leaves in their hats [meaning] the Kings have been reconciled . . .'

18 (1907). Karen Lindahl as one of Astrid's four handmaidens (18.4.1907); Act I: '. . . Astrid, Svend's lovely daughter, approaches, accompanied by her [four] playmates. All surround the king's daughter with expressions of love and admiration . . .'

19 (1920). Karl Merrild as Knud (5.10.1920); Act I: '. . . A ship comes alongside; it is Knud, who has come to Roskilde at Svend's invitation . . . Intensely moved, Knud stands upon the beloved coast of Sjælland . . . with the green bough [of peace] in his hand he waves to the people . . .'

20 (c. 1870). Ludvig Gade as Svend (19.10.1853); Act I:
'. . . Svend enters! Knud can hardly conceal his emotion upon seeing his old opponent again, but overcoming his rancour, he holds out to him the hand of reconciliation . . . Svend gives him an ambiguous look, turns to his halberdiers, and asks how they feel about the King's enemies . . .'

21 (1861). Waldemar Price as Ditleif, leader of Svend's halberdiers (19.12.1857); Act I:
'. . . Wild enthusiasm and crushing gestures throughout the entire host betoken revenge and manslaughter . . . the joyous hope is extinct, the old rancour flares up anew . . .'

22 (c. 1870). Waldemar Price as Waldemar (21.11.1866); Act I:
'. . . It is Waldemar! The mediator of peace! Hearts once again beat warmly . . .'

SCENEBILLEDE FRA BALLETTEN „VALDEMAR"

22.

23 (1901). Oscar Iversen as Svend (26.12.1901), Christian Zangenberg as Axel Hvide (8.12.1901), Axel Madsen as Knud (29.1.1893), Hans Beck as Waldemar (29.1.1893); Act I:
'. . . The Emperor commanded that the kingdom [of Denmark] should be divided . . . Waldemar has the duty of making peace and seeing to the division . . . He seizes his arms and swears upon the altar of his native land [the statue of St. Knud]. Knud follows Waldemar's example, but Svend holds back. Furious, he grips the hilt of his sword, and his devoted halberdiers searchingly await a sign from his hand . . .'

24 (1881). Foreground figures: Arnold Walbom as Ditleif (16.9.1873), Ludvig Gade as Svend (19.10.1853), Marie Westberg as Astrid (22.9.1872), Carl Price as Axel Hvide (16.9.1873), Waldemar Price as Waldemar (21.11.1866), Peter Jerndorff as Knud (4.6.1872); Act I:
'. . . But Astrid and her maidens glide among the fierce warriors; swords and battle-axes are entwined with garlands . . . a shrill of delight surges through the jubilant assembly . . .'

25 (1901). Act II: '. . . The great hall of the royal castle in Roskilde. In the background, trophies from [the battles of] Thostrup and Viborg (Knud's defeat); to the right a throne; to the left a chessboard . . .'

26 (1893). Waldemar Price as Svend (29.1.1893); Act II:
'. . . Sullen and pensive, Ditleif is leaning against the chessboard. Svend sits down and looks fixedly at the chieftain; he then tests the edge of his dagger and hands it to Ditleif . . .'

27 (1907). Holger Holm as Ditleif (18.4.1907); Act II:
'. . . Ditleif takes it, in doubt as to the king's actual intention. But when Svend passes his hand over the chessboard, picks up the King, and holds it out to him, he understands everything. He gives a prearranged signal . . .'

28 (c. 1866). Betty Schnell as Astrid (21.11.1866); Act II:
'. . . Astrid, who has inadvertently witnessed these mysterious doings [at the chess-board], steps forth, pale and trembling, and stops Svend, who does not suspect that she has seen what transpired . . .'

29 (c. 1866). (cont.) '. . . But her alarm, the confusion that drives her now to the chessboard, now to the exits, leaves [Svend] in no doubt as to the fact that he has been betrayed . . .'

30 (c. 1872). Marie Westberg as Astrid (22.9.1872); Act II:
'. . . Astrid does not fear [Svend's] wrath; she implores him for the sake of his honour, of his salvation, to abandon his vengeful purpose . . .'

31 (c.1893). Valborg Jørgensen as Astrid (1.2.1893); Act II:
'. . . She shows him the peace treaty [with Knud and Waldemar] he has sworn to uphold; but this only increases his indignation . . .'

32 (1907). Grethe Ditlevsen as one of Astrid's Ladies-in-waiting (18.4.1907); Act II: '. . . The court gathers . . . Svend goes to meet the kings [Knud and Waldemar] and takes them to the highseat from which he gives a signal for the festivities to begin. Dancing [by four of Astrid's Ladies-in-waiting] . . .'

33 (1904). Ellen Price de Plane as Astrid (17.11.1902); Act II *Pas de deux*: '. . . Waldemar dances with Astrid. He is carried away and does not see all the signs with which she seeks to warn him [against Svend's murderous plot] . . .'

34 (1907). Holger Holm as Ditleif (18.4.1907) and Gustav Uhlendorff as Waldemar (18.4.1907); Act II: '. . . Waldemar beckons the gentlemen [of Knud's suite] and leads them up to the table, where the cups shall be filled anew and drunk to Knud's health . . .'

35 (1907). (cont.) '. . . The signal is given! The hour has come! From every side Svend's halberdiers hurl themselves at the defenceless victims . . .'

36 (1907). (cont.) '. . . Death and destruction rain upon them and many are run through before they can defend themselves . . . Waldemar in the midst of the confusion is fighting with arms he has wrested from the assassins . . .'

37 (1907). (cont.) '. . . Waldemar has seen his last man fall and fights like a tiger against [Ditleif and] the gathering horde . . .'

38 (1907). (cont.) '. . . with gigantic strength he grabs Ditleif . . . The chieftain is forced to the ground . . . No one can conquer the formidable warrior. He cuts his way through the body of men and is pursued by the whole band of assassins . . .'

39 (1920). Karl Merrild as Knud (5.10.1920); Act II: '. . . Axel [Hvide] sees Knud overwhelmed by the traitors and is about to run to his aid; but Knud falls to the ground mortally wounded . . .'

40 (1907). Gustav Uhlendorff as Waldemar (18.4.1907); Act III:
'. . . Wounded and exhausted, he has escaped death . . . his pursuers are close by, but they will not take him alive! He turns his sword on himself. Thunder rolls over his head [as] a sign from Heaven . . . he lays aside the steel and prays . . .'

41 (c.1893). Valborg Jørgensen as Astrid (1.2.1893); Act III:
'. . . Svend enters followed by Astrid. He asks about the fugitives, but his anger mounts with each new report . . . He looks at Astrid suspiciously, but she tries to pacify and soften him . . .'

42 (1904). Ellen Price de Plane as Astrid (17.11.1902); Act III:
'. . . by pointing at the beech leaves, symbol of peace and reconciliation between the kings . . .'

43 (1920). Elna Jørgen-Jensen as Astrid (5.10.1920); Act III:
'. . . She kneels before the image of the saint [Knud], which is illuminated by white tapers [and prays for Waldemar's safe escape] . . .'

44 (1907). Gustav Uhlendorff as Waldemar (18.4.1907); Act III:
'. . . Waldemar appears in full armour . . . Astrid implores the king to evade his enemies. [He] climbs into the boat, and puts off from land, tossing his steel gauntlet onto the coast of Sjælland as a parting gesture . . .'

45 (1907). Holger Holm as Ditleif (18.4.1907); Act III:
'. . . The halberdiers flock to the spot, discover the steel gauntlet and deliver it to the king [Svend]. Ditleif accuses Astrid of having abetted Waldemar's escape. Svend hears this with mounting rage . . .'

46 (1904). Ellen Price de Plane as Astrid (17.11.1902); Act III:
'. . . and when she fearlessly thanks Heaven for the Nobleman's deliverance, [Svend] draws his sword on his own daughter . . .'

47 (1893). Waldemar Price as Svend (29.1.1893) and Anna Harboe as Astrid (29.1.1893); Act III:
'. . . [Svend's] men rush around him; he shatters the blade, but repudiates and curses the unhappy Astrid . . .'

48 (1901). Act IV: '... Grathe Heath [to the right Waldemar's tent; centre stage a granite boulder beyond which is a pillar on which Waldemar is raised above his soldiers in the final tableau (see no. 60)] ...'

49 (1893). Waldemar Price as Svend (29.1.1893); Act IV:
'... [The battle at Grathe Heath] Svend, in full armour, is standing on a stone, surrounded by his bodyguard and esquires: he is watching the battle, which is raging some distance away ...'

50 (1920). Elna Jørgen-Jensen as Astrid disguised as a young esquire in Svend's suite (5.10.1920); Act IV:
'... The esquire follows his lord [in the battle] ...'

51 (1920). Act IV, The battle at Grathe Heath:
The armies of Svend (upstage group) and Waldemar (downstage group) with Nicolai Neiiendam in the centre of the upstage group as Svend (5.10.1920).

52 (c. 1870). Waldemar Price as Waldemar (21.11.1866); Act IV, Grathe Heath:
'. . . The tumult of battle draws closer and it is Waldemar with his men who are advancing . . .'

53 (1907). Holger Holm as Ditleif (18.4.1907); Act IV:
'. . . The fugitives become more numerous; finally Ditleif, too, falls with the standard . . .'

17

54 (1907). Gustav Uhlendorff as Waldemar (18.4.1907) and Holger Holm as Ditleif (18.4.1907); Act IV:
'. . . Waldemar, at the head of a picked troop, falls upon them with crushing force . . . The standard is trampled in the dust, and Svend [and Ditleif], mortally wounded, lie among the vanquished . . .'

55 (1904). Ellen Price de Plane as Astrid, disguised as an esquire (17.11.1902); Act IV:
'. . . [The esquire has] hastened to the aid of his lord. He is the only one who has remained loyal to Svend. He . . . quenches the dying man's thirst. Svend eagerly drinks from the youth's helmet; but when he raises his eyes he sees long curls hanging down over the lad's shoulders . . .'

56 (c. 1893). Valborg Jørgensen as Astrid (1.2.1893); Act IV:
'. . . [Svend] starts back in amazement and recognises Astrid! He releases her from his curse; she is the angel at the gates of eternity . . .'

57 (c. 1871). Betty Schnell as Astrid (21.11.1866); Act IV:
'. . . Astrid forbids [the peasants] to touch her dead father's body. They do not recognise her and are about to use force against the defiant esquire . . .'

58 (c. 1893). Valborg Jørgensen as Astrid (1.2.1893); Act IV: '. . . The peasants withdraw. Astrid takes the standard and lays it at the victor's [Waldemar's] feet. She asks for a grave for her deceased father . . .'

59 (c. 1893). Valborg Jørgensen as Astrid (1.2.1893); Act IV: '. . . Waldemar grants her request . . . When he turns back to Astrid, he starts at seeing her dressed in the garb of the convent. There will her soul repose; there will she pray for her deceased father and bless Waldemar . . . Astrid follows her father's bier . . .'

60 (1920). Gustav Uhlendorff (centre) as Waldemar (5.10.1920) surrounded by soldiers, knights, commanders and prelates; Act IV: '. . . Everyone's eyes are on Waldemar, who is destined to bear the appellation "The Great" . . . All Danes are brothers. Peace and unity shall consolidate the kingdom . . . Waldemar now receives the crown. He is acclaimed, and, hoisted on shields, he enthusiastically surveys his loyal and devoted people . . .'

19

La Sylphide

Romantic Ballet in 2 Acts.
Music by Herman Severin von Løvenskjold.
Scenery by Arnold Wallich.
Costumes by Johan Christian Ryge, adapted from the Paris version as designed by Eugène Lami.
Premiered on November 28, 1836.
Still in repertory.
Number of performances by June 1986: 601.

During a visit to Paris in the summer of 1834 Bournonville saw Adolphe Nourrit's and Filippo Taglioni's *La Sylphide* (premiered at the Paris Opéra on March 12, 1832), which more than any other ballet sealed the triumph of Romanticism in the field of ballet.

On this visit Bournonville was accompanied by his pupil, the fifteen-year-old Lucile Grahn, for whom he immediately decided to mount the ballet in Copenhagen. Due to financial difficulties in obtaining the rights to Jean Schneitzhoeffer's original score, Bournonville commissioned a new score from the young Norwegian composer (and Baron) Herman Severin von Løvenskjold. This provided him with an excellent opportunity to choreograph the title rôle with the specific talent of Lucile Grahn in mind, as well as to bring the rôle of James Reuben (performed by himself) much more into prominence than was the case in Taglioni's original work.

In Copenhagen *La Sylphide* was given completely new scenery (very rare for a ballet at that time) and achieved immense success, in spite of the rather poor number of sylphs in Act II and the primitive stage machinery, compared to that of the impressive Paris version. The ballet has ever since been a milestone for every young ballerina of the Royal Danish Ballet, the only company in the world to have had the ballet in continous repertory since the 1830s.

In France *La Sylphide* inspired the writers Ernest Jaime and Jules Sevèste

to produce a strange but most interesting two-act drama (premiered at Théâtre Montmartre on September 20, 1832), the text and dialogues of which are important sources, as it seems to have kept extremely close to the original mime text of Taglioni's ballet.

In Italy, where in 1828 Louis Henry had created a ballet on the same theme, *La Silfide, ovvero Il Genio dell'aria* (Milan, La Scala, May 28, 1828), Taglioni's ballet was soon adapted by a great number of choreographers. The Italian versions, however, were usually given a stronger mythological accent, thereby becoming a strange mixture of Taglioni's Scottish legend and Henry's Ancient Greek setting. One Italian production by Davide Costa (1856) went so far as to have the ballet played in full Chinese setting. Moreover, nearly all the Italian versions were given a celestial happy ending, showing the Sylph and James united within a final *tableau vivant* in the Olympian spheres.

In Copenhagen the ballet was always kept close to Taglioni's story and Scottish setting, while the dances for the main part had new choreography devised by Bournonville. Of these, the divertissement of the sylphs in Act II was completely rechoreographed by Bournonville for the production on February 4, 1865.

Among the numerous photographs available for *La Sylphide*, a unique series of thirty pictures known to have been taken in September 1903 stands out. It covers the ballet's action from the opening scene right through to the end, featuring Ellen Price de Plane as the Sylphide – a rôle she learned personally from Bournonville's favourite ballerina Juliette Price, who had danced it from 1849 to 1859 – and the youthful twenty-eight-year-old Gustav Uhlendorff as James. Other photographs of specific interest are of the two sets (nos. 61, 86), of which the first was kept almost unchanged for nearly ninety years from the 1836 premiere to the production on March 13, 1924.

61 (1903?). Act I: '. . . A spacious room in a farmhouse. In the background, a door and a staircase leading to the sleeping chamber. To the right, a window. To the left, a high fireplace. Dawn . . .'

62 (1903). Gustav Uhlendorff as James (2.9.1903) and Ellen Price de Plane as the Sylphide (2.9.1903); Act I:
'. . . James is asleep in a large armchair. A feminine being in airy raiment and with transparent wings is kneeling at his feet
. . . With her hand beneath her chin, she fixes her loving gaze on the sleeping youth . . .'

63 (1866). Juliette Price as the Sylphide (22.9.1849); Act I:
'. . . She expresses the joy she feels in being near the one she loves . . .'

64 (1905). Ellen Price de Plane as the Sylphide (2.9.1903); Act I:
'. . . She hovers around him and flutters her wings in order to cool the air he breathes . . .'

65 (1905). (cont.)

66 (1905). (cont.)

67 (1903). Gustav Uhlendorff as James (2.9.1903) and Ellen Price de Plane as the Sylphide (2.9.1903); Act I:
'. . . James slumbers restlessly. In his dreams he follows every one of the air creature's movements, and when, carried away with tenderness, she approaches him lightly and kisses his brow . . .'

68 (1903). (cont.) '. . . he suddenly wakens . . .'

69 (1903). (cont.) '. . . reaches out to grasp the lovely image, and pursues it about the room as far as the fireplace, into which the Sylphide vanishes . . .'

70 (1918). Magda Tvergaard as Effy (11.10.1917) and Aage Eibye as Gurn (4.6.1918); Act I:
'. . . Effy is brought in by her aunt . . . Gurn . . . is immediately at her service. He begs her not to reject the spoils of the hunt and gives her a bouquet of fresh wildflowers . . .'

71 (1895). Anna Harboe as Madge (28.9.1895); Act I:
'. . . [James:] "What are you doing here?" [Madge:] "I am warming myself by the fire." [James:] "Get away from here, witch! Your presence is an evil omen." James is about to drive her away, but the girls plead for her . . .'

72 (1903). Gustav Uhlendorff as James (2.9.1903), Valborg Guldbrandsen as Effy (2.9.1903), Hans Beck as Madge (2.9.1903), corps de ballet as Scottish peasants, and, at far right, Christian Christensen as Gurn (2.9.1903); Act I:
'. . . Madge knows hidden things, and the girls cannot resist their desire to know what lies in store for them. They surround the witch and hold out their hands to have her predict their fortunes . . . Finally, Effy asks if she will be happy in marriage. "Yes!" is the answer. "Does my bridegroom love me sincerely?" "No!" . . .'

73 (1903). Hans Beck as Madge (2.9.1903), Valborg Guldbrandsen as Effy (2.9.1903), Gustav Uhlendorff as James (2.9.1903); Act I:
'. . . James now becomes furious [at Madge's prophecy to Effy], seizes the fortune-teller, and hurls her to the door . . .'

74 (1918). Christian Borgen as John, James's father (12.12.1913), Magda Tvergaard as Effy (11.10.1917), Harry Larsen as James (3.11.1917), Aage Eiby as Gurn (4.6.1918); Act I:
'. . . Gurn quotes [Madge's] utterance and makes yet another effort to hinder the wedding he detests so much . . .'

75 (1871). Marie Westberg as the Sylphide (6.9.1871); Act I:
'. . . as if by a gust of wind the casement opens. The Sylphide is in the corner, melancholy and hiding her face in her hands . . .'

76 (1903). Gustav Uhlendorff as James (2.9.1903) and Ellen Price de Plane as the Sylphide (2.9.1903); Act I:
'. . . James bids her approach, and she glides from the wall . . .'

77 (1903). (cont.) '. . . He asks the cause of her grief, but she refuses to answer . . .'

78 (1903). (cont.) '. . . When he continues to demand her confidence, she finally confesses that his union with Effy constitutes her misfortune . . . James has listened to her with mounting agitation. He is touched by the Sylphide's love, but does not dare to return it . . . he shudders at the thought of deserting Effy . . .'

79 (1903). (cont.) '. . . tears himself loose from the Sylphide, and spurns her . . .'

80 (1903). (cont.) '. . . But the Sylphide has wrapped herself in Effy's plaid, and when he turns around he finds her at his feet, reminding him of his beloved. James is enchanted at this sight . . .'

81 (1903). (cont.) '. . . Gurn, who has witnessed part of the foregoing scene, hastens to acquaint Effy with everything that has happened, but when James hears a noise he hides the Sylphide in the armchair and covers her with the plaid . . .'

82 (1904). Karl Merrild as a young Scottish peasant (16.1.1909); Act I: '. . . All the villagers arrive to celebrate the betrothal of James and Effy. The old folk sit down at table, while the young ones enjoy merry dancing [here the second man's variation today known as James's solo] . . .'

83 (1909). Poul Witzansky as a Scottish child (Season 1908–09); Act I, *The Reel*.

84 (1904). Ellen Price de Plane as the Sylphide (2.9.1903) and Gustav Uhlendorff as James (2.9.1903); Act I: '. . . James alone is melancholy. He stands apart from the others with the betrothal ring in his hand. The Sylphide emerges from the fireplace, snatches the ring from him . . .'

85 (1904). (cont.) '. . . and indicates with an expression of utter despair that she must die if he marries Effy. [Overwhelmed, James follows her into the forest] . . .'

86 (c.1903?). Act II: '. . . The forest at night. A dense fog permits only a glimpse of the foremost trees and cliffs. To the left, the entrance to a cave . . .'

87 (c.1882). Hans Beck as James (5.2.1882); Act II: '. . . The Sylphide leads James down from a steep mountain path . . . This is her domain. Here she will live for the one she loves . . . and allow him to share the joys she prizes so highly. James is enraptured with delight and admiration . . .'

88 (1913). Elna Jørgen-Jensen as the Sylphide (12.12.1913); Act II: '. . . The Sylphide seems to fathom his every desire, brings him the loveliest flowers . . .'

89 (1903). Ellen Price de Plane as the Sylphide (2.9.1903) and Gustav Uhlendorff as James (2.9.1903); Act II:
'... and refreshes him with fruits and spring water. James regards her with rapture. He forgets everything for the one he loves, and lives and breathes only to possess her...'

90 (c. 1882). Hans Beck as James (5.2.1882); Act II:
'... But she is more retiring than usual. She will not sit with him, easily disengages herself from his arms, and eludes him every time he ardently tries to embrace her. James is on the verge of becoming annoyed...'

91 (1882). Anna Tychsen as the Sylphide (5.2.1882); Act II:
'... but then she hovers about him in the most delightful attitudes... The Sylphide perceives his state of mind and seeks to dispel his dark thoughts with her innocent merriment...'

92 (1908). Agnes Nyrop as The First Sylphide (2.9.1903); Act II:
'... She knows a way: her sisters shall help her to cheer her beloved. At a signal they all come into view through bushes, on boughs, and over the cliffs. Young sylphides with wings of blue and rose soon chase away the youth's distress...'

93 (1903). Ellen Price de Plane as the Sylphide (2.9.1903) and Gustav Uhlendorff as James (2.9.1903) surrounded by corps de ballet; Act II:
'. . . Their dancing and delightful groupings arouse James's enthusiasm. He is more than ever taken with the Sylphide, but she eludes his embraces and, after having disappointed him several times disappears the very moment he thought to grasp her . . .'

94 (1918). Aage Eibye as Gurn (4.6.1918), Karl Merrild as Madge (4.6.1918), Magda Tvergaad as Effy (11.10.1917); Act II:
'. . . James's friends come into view on the hill. Gurn is with them . . . Madge now tells them of [James's] unfaithfulness. He is lost to Effy, but her prophecy will be fulfilled; for Gurn . . . is destined by fate to be Effy's husband . . .'

95 (1903). Hans Beck as Madge (2.9.1903); Act II:
'. . . Old Madge has been watching [James] secretly and approaches [the veil hidden on her back] with feigned compassion . . . [Madge:] "But the one you love is a sylphide! Naught save a talisman can bind her to you" . . .'

96 (1905). Gustav Uhlendorff as James (2.9.1903); Act II:
'. . . "Give it to me! In return I will bestow upon you all that I possess" . . . Madge
suffers herself to be moved and meaningfully hands him the rose-coloured scarf
. . . Beside himself with joy and gratitude, James kisses the scarf . . .'

97 (c. 1871). Marie Westberg as the Sylphide (6.9.1871); Act II:
'. . . He spies the Sylphide on a bough with a bird's nest in her hands . . .'

98 (c. 1892–95). Valborg Jørgensen as the Sylphide (24.11.1892); Act II:
'. . . She climbs down and offers him her catch, but James reproaches her for being
harsh toward innocent creatures. Deeply moved, she regrets what she has done and
hastens to replace the nest . . .'

31

99 (c. 1882). Anna Tychsen as the Sylphide (5.2.1882) and Hans Beck as James (5.2.1882); Act II:
'. . . He waves the scarf . . . She now pleads for the pretty scarf, which he purposely refuses her. She begs him for it . . .'

100 (1903). Ellen Price de Plane as the Sylphide (2.9.1903) and Gustav Uhlendorff as James (2.9.1903); Act II:
'. . . Greedily, she reaches for the scarf . . .'

101 (1903). (cont.) '. . . but at the same instant he twists it about her so tightly that she cannot move her arms. The Sylphide is captured and, kneeling, asks for mercy . . .'

102 (1903). (cont.) '. . . James, who had thought to possess her forever and in his outburst of joy gives her a thousand caresses, suddenly stops . . .'

103 (1881). Marie Westberg as the Sylphide (6.9.1871); Act II: '. . . The unhappy creature! By taking away her freedom he has robbed her of life . . .'

104 (1903). Gustav Uhlendorff as James (2.9.1903) and Ellen Price de Plane as the Sylphide (2.9.1903); Act II: '. . . but James does not release the scarf until her wings have fallen off . . .'

105 (1903). (cont.) '. . . He throws himself at her feet . . . the pallor of death covers the Sylphide's brow . . . "Do not weep! You, whom I have so dearly loved! I was blessed by your tenderness, but I could not belong to you, could not give you the happiness you longed for . . .'

The Festival in Albano

Idyllic Ballet in 1 Act.
Music by Johannes Frederik Fröhlich and Iohan Peter Emilius Hartmann (*pas de deux*).
Scenery by Christian Ferdinand Christensen.
Costumes by August Bournonville, partly adapted from older repertory (*La Muette de Portici*).
Premiered on October 28, 1839.
Last performance: December 27, 1919 (an extended version with incorporated dances from *The Flower Festival in Genzano* and *Pas de la Vestale* was reconstructed by Elsa Marianne von Rosen and premiered on February 1, 1961, in Kalmar (Sweden) in a touring programme for the Scandinavian Ballet).
Number of performances by 1919: 151.

The Festival in Albano was Bournonville's first 'Italian' ballet, created two years before he actually visited that country. The ballet, merely a divertissement, achieved much success, mainly because it was an affectionate tribute to the Danish sculptor Bertel Thorvaldsen, who had returned to his native country in 1838 after many years in Rome.

In the spring of 1839 Bournonville had visited the annual art exhibition at Charlottenborg Palace to see the new works by Danish painters who had returned from Italy. He immediately found inspiration for a genre ballet in Albert Küchler's 'Scene with a family in Albano' as well as a painting by the Italian painter Luigi Fiorini called 'Scene from a Roman *osteria* with the host performing as improvisator' (both today in the Thorvaldsen Gallery, Copenhagen). These paintings together suggested a plot, which centres on a young Italian bridal couple and a Danish artist, the latter unwittingly causing the jealousy and wrath of the young bridegroom by secretly having painted a portrait of his future wife. All conflicts are happily resolved, however, and the ballet ends with joy and dancing, during which a series of *tableaux vivants* are shown, representing some of Thorvaldsen's most classic sculptures.

In spite of the lasting popularity of this short ballet only a few photographs are available, of which two (nos. 108, 109) show the ballet's choreographic centrepiece, the technically extremely demanding pas de deux, which was performed by a young couple disguised as Bacchus and Venus. This dance was later described by Bournonville as 'a pas de deux containing attitudes from ancient and modern sculptures', and was reinserted for dancer Anna Scholl in the first production of the ballet after Bournonville's death, given on December 3, 1882. However, it was only performed for that season, after which it was omitted until the ballet's last production in 1919, when it was rechoreographed by dancer Emilie Walbom, only to disappear with the ballet's last performance on December 27 the same year.

106 (1919). The scene is set in Albano, three miles south of Rome.
'. . . An elevated open square from which, through the town and some pieces of luxuriant vegetation, one looks out over the *Campagna* to Rome. To the right, Vincenza's [Silvia's mother's] house; to the left, the inn, on which can be read: *Osteria con Cucina*. Between the two houses, a flight of stairs [leads] from the terrace down into the valley. In the right foreground, a picture of the Madonna is fastened to an old evergreen oak . . .'

107 (1919). Elna Jørgen-Jensen as Silvia (14.5.1919):
'. . . Vincenza leads her daughter [Silvia] down to her childhood playground in the shade of the evergreen oak, beneath the gentle gaze of the Madonna. Here she will receive her bridal array – the white veil, the bouquet of orange blossoms – and from here . . . she shall go to meet her unknown fate . . .'

108 (1919). Karl Merrild as Bacchus (14.5.1919): *Pas de deux*
'. . . visiting pilgrims are announced . . . They swiftly cast off their hats and cloaks, emerging in the new guise of Bacchus and Venus. In a *pas de deux* containing attitudes from ancient and modern sculptures, they salute the festival's favourites: Bacchus offers his thyrus to the young winegrower [Antonio] . . .'

109 (c 1882) Anna Tychsen as Venus (3.12.1882): *Pas de deux*
'. . . while Venus presents her golden apple to the lovely bride [Silvia] . . .'

The Toreador

Idyllic Ballet in 2 Acts.

Music composed and arranged by Edvard Helsted.

Scenery by Christian Ferdinand Christensen.

Costumes by August Bournonville, partly adapted from older repertory.

Premiered on November 27, 1840.

Last performance: December 8, 1929 (a freely adapted version with choreography by Flemming Flindt to a score arranged by Erling D. Bjerno was premiered on March 17, 1978. This version was revived for the Royal Swedish Ballet (Stockholm) the same year, and for the Dallas Ballet, Texas, in 1983).

Number of performances by 1929: 251.

In the months of June and July, 1840, the famous Spanish dancers of the time Mariano Camprubí and Dolores Serral gave a series of performances at Copenhagen's Royal Theatre, including the popular Spanish dances *El Jaleo de Xerxes*, *La Jota Arragones*, *Las Machegas de la Pia* and *El Bolero*, among others. Of these dances, *El Bolero* was extended on July 6, 1840, to be performed by two couples, now retitled *El Bolero à quatre* and with Bournonville and Caroline Fjeldsted performing as the second couple. This experience, together with the enormous enthusiasm with which the citizens of Copenhagen received these Spanish dances, fired Bournonville with inspiration for a two-act ballet on a Spanish theme, in which the *Bolero à quatre* was to be incorporated as the Finale.

The ballet, premiered only four months after the visit of the Spanish dancers, received an extraordinary success and lasting popularity. Together with his later masterpiece *Napoli* (choreographed the following year), *The Toreador* became one of the most often performed ballets during Bournonville's lifetime.

To create a true Spanish setting and atmosphere as seen through foreign eyes, Bournonville made up a plot with two English tourists, who visit a small village outside Madrid. Later the village is also visited by Céleste, a *danseuse* from the Paris Opéra who is passing through en route for Madrid, where she intends to give a series of farewell performances. The three foreigners get involved with the life of the local villagers, provoking a number of intrigues and baroque situations. Moreover, by having the French *danseuse* perform some of the highlights from the Paris Opéra repertory in the midst of the local Spaniards, Bournonville succeeded in emphasising the true Spanish national dances by juxtaposing them with the pure academic style of the French Romantic Ballet.

However, for the ballet's last production in 1929, Elna Jørgen-Jensen and Harald Lander considerably increased the number of Spanish dances by adding five new ones to Bournonville's original three, thus spoiling the carefully balanced interplay between the Spanish national dances and the dance of the French academic school, as originally envisaged by Bournonville. Being now turned into a sort of Spanish national dance display, the ballet lost most of its original choreographic concept and soon went out of the repertory.

The photographic sources available for *The Toreador* cover a performance period of more than seventy years (1856–1929), thus clearly revealing the stylistic changes and development of the Spanish ballet costume in that period (exemplified in particular by no. 132 compared with 133 & 134).

110 (1929). Act I: '. . . The courtyard and garden of an inn. In the background, a wall, broken through in several places and almost completely covered with ivy and vines . . .'

111 (c.1905). Ellen Braunstein as Maria (18.2.1904); Act I:
'. . . when [Pedro] sees Maria so dejected [longing for her lover Alonzo's return] he gives her a flower with which to bid the triumphant Alonzo welcome . . .'

112 (c. 1881–87). Athalia Flammé as Maria (11.5.1881); Act I:
'. . . and together with Paquitta [Pedro] dances [a merry *zapateado*] to distract and cheer Maria . . .'

113 (c. 1884). Hans Beck as Alonzo (13.2.1884); Act I.

114 (1911). Poul Huld as Mr Arthur (13.5.1911) and Christian Christensen as Mr William (13.5.1911); Act I:
'. . . Arthur and William, two rich [English] gentlemen, who have wagered for and against Alonzo [at the bullfight in Madrid] have followed the [returning] crowd [to José's inn] . . .'

115 (1929). Aage Fønss as Mr Arthur (22.3.1929) and Carl Madsen as Mr William (22.3.1929); Act I:
'. . . [in playing dice] the jolly Mr William has won his melancholy countryman's money. He is indescribably happy . . .'

116 (c. 1864–70). Harald Scharff as Alonzo (28.3.1864); Act I:
'. . . Alonzo arrives for his rendezvous [with Maria]. Tonight is the last time he will stand [serenading] outside Maria's window as her lover. Tomorrow he will lead her home as his bride . . .'

117 (c. 1881). Waldemar Price as Alonzo (28.11.1873); Act I:
'. . . Maria now wishes to learn what happened at the bullfight which all the others witnessed. Alonzo is instantly willing to describe it . . . MIMED MONOLOGUE: Alonzo now appears as himself . . . Everyone admires his bearing and the calmness with which he enters the ring . . .'

118 (1899). Adolph Frederik Lense as Mr William (13.2.1884); Act I:
Mr William takes part in Alonzo's narration of the bullfight by posing as a Toreador with a red scarf in front of the fuming 'bull'.

119 (1911). Gustav Uhlendorff as Don Alonzo (13.5.1911); Act I:
'. . . Everyone is tense with expectation. The bull roars within its enclosure; it is bated with dagger tips . . . In a picturesque pose he awaits the third charge, then thrusts his sword into the bull's chest, seizes it by the horns, forces the bull to the ground, and slays it with his dagger . . .'

120 (1904). Ellen Price de Plane as Maria (24.1.1904); Act I:
'. . . Thunderous applause hails the victor . . . Alonzo runs about the ring amid general admiration. He presents to his beloved the golden chain he has won [in the real bullfight] and as he rapturously embraces her he is greeted with heartfelt sympathy from every side . . .'

121 (1911). Grethe Ditlevsen as Céleste (13.5.1911); Act I:
'. . . The sound of wagon wheels and the cracking of a whip is heard. A post chaise is driven into the backyard . . . the guests curiously gather at the gate. It is two ladies: a young [Céleste] and an old one [Mme Finard, her mother], very distinguished looking . . .'

122 (c. 1861). Petrine Fredstrup as Maria (17.6.1856); Act I, *El Jaleo de Xeres*:
'. . . The young villagers are rather shy, but José [the innkeeper] orders dancing to begin and guitars, tambourines and castanets are immediately set in motion . . .'

123 (1904). Ellen Price de Plane as Maria (24.1.1904); Act I, *El Jaleo de Xeres*:
'. . . The young lady [Céleste], who . . . has only now and then deigned to peer at the dancers through her lorgnette, beomes ever more attentive to the charming *Jaleo* performed by Alonzo and Maria with all the enthusiasm of a couple in love . . .'

124 (1889). Anna Tychsen as Céleste (11.5.1881); Act I:
'. . . As airy as a sylphide in a light, short dress, [Céleste] glides into the astonished villagers' midst . . .'

125 (1911). Grethe Ditlevsen as Céleste (13.5.1911); Act I:
'. . . It is no longer the affected young lady but [the *danseuse*] Mademoiselle Céleste, who is travelling from Paris [where she recently has retired from the Paris Opéra] to Madrid and intends to capture all hearts with her motto: "*Je suis la bayadère [de la Danse]*!" . . .'

126 (1904). Ellen Price de Plane as Maria (24.1.1904), Act I:
'. . . Maria, in despair over Alonzo's sudden imprisonment [caused by the jealous Mr William], rushes over to Céleste to tell her that William is to blame for her bridegroom's misfortune . . .'

127 (1929). Act II (from March 22, 1929 with an original scenery):
'. . . The road to Madrid runs past the gate, and on the far side of the roadway can be seen a magnificent landscape bordered by distant mountains and a brook which flows through the ruins of a Roman acqueduct . . .'

128 (1911). Poul Huld as Mr Arthur (13.5.1911), Ella Jacobsen as Mme Finard (13.5.1911), Grethe Ditlevsen as Césèste (13.5.1911); Act II:
'. . . The suitor [Mr Arthur] does not immediately grasp the meaning [of Céleste's refusals to his repeated proposals of marriage], but soon perceives that it concerns a definite refusal. His [feigned] despair knows no bounds. He threatens to kill himself if his request is not granted . . . The frightened Céleste swoons . . .'

129 (1899). Adolph Frederik Lense as Mr William (13.2.1884); Act II:
'. . . Everything is ready for [Mr Arthur's] perfect abduction [of Céleste] when William suddenly rushes in, stops the horses, and summons the crowd of people returning with the [newly released] Toreador . . . A frightful commotion arises: . . . William thrashes the coachman and the jockey . . .'

130 (1911). Ella Jacobsen as Mme Finard (13.5.1911), Grethe Ditlevsen as Céléste (13.5.1911), Christian Christensen as Mr William (13.5.1911); Act II:
'... William's joviality and heartiness, his earlier and better-thought-out proposal [to Céléste], his speed in preventing the abduction, and especially his obtaining Alonzo's release have given him an essential advantage over his rival. Her mother gives the union her blessing ... William is in seventh heaven ...'

131 (1911). Grethe Ditlevsen as Céléste (13.5.1911); Act II:
'... Céléste, who will now leave the theatre and, with a sort of sadness, bid farewell to her airy art, wishes to see once more the Spaniards' lovely dancing ...'

132 (c. 1861). Petrine Fredstrup as Maria (17.6.1856); Act II, *Bolero à quatre*:
'... At [Céléste's] behest the lightest couple [Maria and Alonzo – later joined by Paquitta and Pedro] perform a lovely and graceful *bolero* [*à quartre*] ...'

133 (c. 1881). Charlotte Schousgaard as Paquitta (11.5.1881); Act II, *Bolero à quatre*.

134 (1909). Grethe Ditlevsen (Summer 1909), Richard Jensen (10.11.1906), Elna Lauesgaard (Summer 1909), Gustav Uhlendorff (24.1.1904); Act II, *Bolero à quatre*.

135 (1909). (cont.) *Bolero à quatre*.

136 (1909). (cont.) *Bolero à quatre*.

Napoli

Romantic Ballet in 3 Acts.
Music by Holger Simon Paulli (Acts I and III), Edvard Helsted (Acts I and III), Niels W. Gade (Act II), and Hans Christian Lumbye (Act III: Finale).
Scenery by Christian Ferdinand Christensen.
Costumes by August Bournonville, partly adapted from older repertory (*La Muette de Portici, The Festival in Albano*).
Premiered on March 29, 1842.
Still in repertory.
Number of performances by June 1986: 648.

Napoli, Bournonville's absolute masterpiece, came into existence thanks to an unfortunate incident which took place in the Royal Theatre in the spring of 1841, when, having created a scandal by involving the absolute monarch in a theatrical dispute, Bournonville was obliged to accept a six-month leave of absence from his position as ballet-master.

During this leave of absence he visited a number of major European cities, of which Naples was to have the most overwhelming impact on his creative mind. During his nine-week stay in the city, his imagination was daily spurred by the picturesque and vivacious Neapolitan street life that surrounded him and which he carefully observed from the fourth-floor balcony of an apartment on the harbour front of Santa Lucia. Later, towards the end of his stay in Naples, he witnessed from a bridge near Portici at the outskirts of Naples the massive return of the inhabitants to the city from a three-day open air Whitsun festival at the nearby sanctuary of the Madonna dell'Arco. Finally, he found inspiration by visiting the famous blue grotto on the isle of Capri as well as by attending a performance at the San Carlo theatre of the three-act ballet *Il Duca di Ravenna*, by his Italian fellow choreographer Salvatore Taglioni. In Act II of this ballet, a scene was included that took place in the blue grotto, depicting the struggles and temptations to which the young Duke of Ravenna is exposed by the naiads, having been shipwrecked on a crusade against the Saracens.

All together, these Neapolitan experiences fired Bournonville with inspiration for a three-act ballet that was fully conceived on his return to Copenhagen in the late autumn of 1841, and given its final form in less than four months, being premiered in March 1842. Since then *Napoli* has been the most often performed Bournonville ballet ever, and represents the true trade-mark of his style with regard to drama, mimic characterisation, and choreography.

Together, the many photographs available for *Napoli* cover a performance period of nearly ninety years, from the ballet's creation in 1842 (no. 151) to the 1928 production (no. 170). They reflect the astonishing scenic continuity of this ballet with regard to both costumes and décor. However, they do also reveal a number of significant differences from today's performances in terms of groupings, postures, and mimic expressiveness (e.g. nos. 143, 153, 158, 167, 170, 173).

137 (1903?). Act I: '. . . The square and beach of Santa Lucia are seen in the glow of lamps, torches and kitchen fires. The bay is shrouded in darkness. TABLEAU: A tent is stretched crosswise above the street so that only the second storeys of the houses are visible. To the left, a staircase leading up to the abode of Veronica [Teresina's mother]; to the right, a palace with light gleaming through its red curtains . . .'

44

138 (1862). Harald Scharff as Gennaro (8.1.1860); Act I:
'... The barcarolle announces the fishermen's return. Everyone gathers round to see their catch. Gennaro rushes over to his beloved [Teresina] ...'

139 (1922). Richard Jensen as Gennaro (2.4.1914) and Elna Jørgen-Jensen as Teresina (16.9.1915); Act I:
'... Veronica [Teresina's mother] allows her child to take part in the dancing [a *Ballabile*] and merriment ...'

140 (1906). Grethe Ditlevsen (5.10.1905); Act I, *Ballabile*.

141 (1908). Holger Mehnen and Poul Petersen as Neapolitan children (18.9.1908); Act I.

142 (1928). Lili Sørensen (far left) as Giovanina (8.1.1926), Aage Eibye (centre) as Pascarillo (16.9.1915) and corps de ballet; Act I: '. . . Pascarillo, the Neapolitans' favourite buffoon and street singer, enters with his musician. Delighted, everyone gathers round him, and with a brilliant recitative he prefaces the treat he intends to give his numerous audience . . .'

143 (c. 1867–76). Frederik Ferdinand Hoppensach as Pascarillo (29.3.1842); Act I.

144 (1909). Christian Christensen as Pascarillo (11.5.1902); Act I.

145 (1915). Karl Merrild as Pascarillo (29.5.1915); Act I.

146 (1867). Harald Scharff as Gennaro (8.1.1860); Act I:
'. . . Filled with renewed hope [of finding the vanished Teresina], Gennaro seizes the anchor, fetches his oars and is about to go whither the monk [Fra Ambrosio] pointed. But the pious father gives him a precious amulet: a picture of the Madonna dell'Arco . . .'

147 (c. 1877–85). Waldemar Price as Gennaro (15.3.1873); Act I:
'. . . This shall aid him in the face of all obstacles, dangers and temptations and defeat any sorcery. Filled with confidence and gratitude, Gennaro sets off . . .'

148 (1903?). Act II: '. . . *Grotta d'azzurra* (the Blue Grotto) on the isle of Capri.
The sea swells constitute a prelude. One sees the empty grotto. Its dark pillars form the foreground; the water, with its magical play of colour, fills up the interior of the cave, and in the far background, sunlight pours in through the low and narrow entrance to the grotto . . .'

47

149 (c. 1898). Waldemar Price as Golfo (29.10.1885), Anna Harboe as Teresina (29.10.1885) and corps de ballet as the naiads; Act II: '. . . a large shell comes drifting in. [The two leading naiads] Argentina and Coralla are holding the lifeless Teresina in their arms. The other [originally ten] naiads crowd around to see the new arrival . . . Golfo is charmed by her beauty . . .'

150 (c. 1885). Anna Jensen as Teresina (29.10 1885); Act II: '. . . Teresina [transformed into a naiad] observes her guitar, but it has lost all meaning for her; she does not know how to play it any more . . . The shrill tones of the conch are more to her liking. She takes up a shell and blows it . . .'

151 (c. 1844). Marie Cathrine Werning as a naiad (29.3.1842); Act II: '. . . and the tritons and naiads perform fantastic dances . . .'

152 (c. 1873–85). Waldemar Price as Gennaro (15.3.1873); Act II:
'. . . Gennaro rows into the grotto . . . Suddenly he notices Teresina's guitar . . .
He tries to play their favourite song . . . but its sounds are displeasing to her . . .'

153 (1862). Andreas Füssel as Golfo (29.3.1842), Act II:
'. . . Golfo halts [Teresina and Gennaro's] escape; his wrath is terrible. Neither pleas
nor tears can soften him . . .'

154 (c. 1885). Anna Jensen as Teresina (29.10.1885); Act II:
'. . . Relying upon the Madonna's aid, she raises the amulet aloft and bids the spirits
of the sea humble themselves before the Queen of Heaven. Golfo, who must yield
to a higher power, now permits Teresina to leave [the blue grotto] with Gennaro . . .'

155 (1903?). Act III: '. . . Monte Vergine outside Naples. A bridge connects one hill to the other. A niche in the centre pillar of the bridge contains a picture of the Madonna, and beneath the large arches can be seen the bay and the shore near Vesuvius. It is midday . . .'

156 (c. 1885). Hans Beck as Gennaro (29.10.1885); Act III: '. . . Gennaro appears, richly dressed. Teresina declares [to the crowd of pilgrims] that it was he who rescued her . . . The idea that witchcraft is involved becomes even more firmly rooted in the minds of the bewildered crowd . . . Bewildered and disgusted by all the occur-rences, the unhappy fisherman flies into a dreadful rage . . .'

157 (1905). Ellen Price de Plane (15.9.1903); Act III, *Pas de six*: '. . . The liveliest dances [*Pas de six* followed by *Tarantella* and a *Bacchanalian Finale*] succeed one another . . .'

158 (1909). Richard Jensen (22.9.1904) and Grethe Ditlevsen (10.5.1907); Act III, *Pas de six*.

159 (1909). Gustav Uhlendorff (10.10.1903) and Elna Lauesgaard (9.1.1907); Act III, *Tarantella* (pas de deux-section with the shawl dance).

160 (c. 1864–71). Laura Juel as Giovanina (7.10.1864); Act III, *Tarantella*.

161 (1928). Vera Liisberg as Teresina (29.12.1928) and Kaj Smith as Gennaro (29.12.1928); Act III, *Tarantella*.

162 (c. 1870). Jeanette Hansen (2.6.1870); Act III, *Tarantella*.

163 (c. 1870). (cont.) *Tarantella*.

164 (1903). Hans Beck as Gennaro (29.10.1885) and Valborg Guldbrandsen as Teresina (28.1.1903); Act III, *Tarantella*.

165 (1903). (cont.) *Tarantella*.

166 (1909). Grethe Ditlevsen (10.5.1907), Richard Jensen (22.9.1904), Elna Lauesgaard (9.1.1907), Gustav Uhlendorff (10.10.1903); Act III, *Tarantella*.

167 (1909). (cont.) *Tarantella*.

168 (1904). Yelva Lange (28.1.1903); Act III, *Bacchanalian Finale*.

169 (1907). Karen Lindahl (10.5.1907); Act III, *Bacchanalian Finale*.

170 (1928). Emma Forchammer (29.12.1928), Leif Ørnberg (8.1.1926), Agnete Tilling (29.12.1928), Knud Højby-Henriksen (8.1.1926), Margrethe Brock-Nielsen (22.6.1922), Svend Aage Larsen (29.12.1928), Bente Hørup-Hassing (22.6.1922), Harry Larsen (22.6.1922), Asta Krum-Hansen (29.12.1928), Svend Carlo Jensen (8.1.1926), Inger Praëm (29.12.1928), Harald Lander (22.6.1922); Act III, Group from *Bacchanalian Finale*.

171 (1902). William Frørup as Neapolitan child (28.1.1903); Act III, *Bacchanalian Finale*.

172 (1905). (cont.)

173 (c. 1898). In the cart: Emilie Walbom as Veronica (30.10.1898), Anna Harboe as Teresina (29.10.1885), Hans Beck as Gennaro (29.10.1885). At each side of the cart: Gustav Uhlendorff and Valborg Guldbrandsen, Ellen Price and Edouard Büchner, and corps de ballet; Act III: '. . . the procession once again sets off to return to Naples. Some young fellows have unhitched the horses from a cart and transform it into a triumphal car for our hero and heroine, who, surrounded by the jubilant throng and crowned with flowers, are driven home amid a bacchanalian finale . . .'

Bellman, or the Polska at Grönalund

Vaudeville-Ballet in 1 Act.
Music partly after Bellman's *Fredmans Epistler*, arranged by Holger Simon Paulli.
Costumes by August Bournonville, partly adapted from older repertory.
Premiered on June 3, 1844.
Last performance: May 29, 1899.
Number of performances: 125.

This ballet, Bournonville's tribute to the popular Swedish poet-songwriter Carl Michael Bellman (1740–1795), draws on familiar characters and melodies from Bellman's famous song collection *Fredman's Epistler*.

Bournonville himself declares that he found inspiration for this ballet in a transparent back-cloth painted by Danish artists Wilhelm Marstrand and Jørgen Sonne as décor for a performance given in Copenhagen by the Scandinavian Society in December 1840 to honour the centenary of Bellman's birth. This may well be true, but the inspiration for this work may just as well stem from the memories and accounts given by Bournonville's father Antoine to his son, about his cheerful youth in the company of this famous Swedish poet during Antoine's years as leading dancer at the court ballet of King Gustav III in Stockholm. Antoine Bournonville died in 1843, and to honour his memory Bournonville seems to have found it most appropriate to depict the artistic milieu in Stockholm described in Bellman's epistles, and in which his father had spent some of his most happy years as a young dancer.

The few photographs available for *Bellman* depict the ballet's leading female character, Ulla Wiinblad, whom the poet Fredman both teases and loves at the same time. The photographs cover a period of nearly twenty-five years of performances (1861–1884) and are, as such, a small but interesting example of how the ballet costume (here a stylised rococo evening gown) was often slightly altered or modified in order to make the dress accord better with the fashion of the time (no. 175 compared with no. 174).

174 (c. 1880–84). Anna Tychsen as Ulla Viinblad (17.12.1880); Scene 2: '. . . [Bellman] asks for wine, improvises on his lute, teases Ulla; and when she gets angry because he has written a ballad about her, he restores her charm and gaiety by giving a representation of the drunken Fredman . . .'

175 (c. 1861). Petrine Fredstrup as Ulla Viinblad (8.9.1846); Scene 4: '. . . The orchestra strikes up and the dancing begins: [Ulla dances] minuet and polska [a popular Swedish dance of Polish origin] . . .'

Conservatoriet, or A Proposal of Marriage through the Newspaper

Vaudeville-Ballet in 2 Acts.
Music arranged and composed by Holger Simon Paulli.
Scenery arranged by Christian Ferdinand Christensen.
Costumes by August Bournonville, partly adapted from older repertory.
Premiered on May 6, 1849.
Last performance: March 5, 1934 (a one-act version with the 'Dancing School' of Act I was premiered on October 24, 1941, and is still in repertory, while a two-act adapted version of the complete ballet was staged by Niels Bjørn Larsen at the Pantomime Theatre in the Tivoli Gardens, Copenhagen, on June 24, 1959).
Number of performances by 1934: 166.

The idea of mounting a two-act contemporary ballet depicting the disciplined everyday life of the dance students at the Paris Opéra, as opposed to the unrestrained hilarity of the students and *grisettes* of Paris on the weekly Sunday excursion to the St. Germain-en-Laye amusement park, must, at first sight, have looked like a most daring project to the management of Copenhagen's Royal Theatre.

However, thanks to Bournonville's special talent for creating lively and picturesque scenes of a natural and catching light-heartedness, the ballet at once received a most favourable reception in spite of its rather thin plot. A critic (*Berlingske Tidende*, May 7, 1849) praised Bournonville's talent for 'depicting how the dull life of the students and the grisettes is transformed into true Parisian *joie de vivre*, when they leave their small studies and humble dressmaker's workrooms and gather at the outskirts of Paris to dance the *Can-Can*, enjoy life, and *pour faire l'amour*.'

Bournonville's intention with this ballet was, however, a rather deeper one. He wanted to pay a tribute to his teacher at the Paris Opéra school, the legendary Auguste Vestris, who had passed away a few years earlier. He therefore incorporated an entire dance lesson in Act I, which, when carefully analysed, proves to contain a large number of exactly the same *enchaînements* that he himself had studied with Vestris in the late 1820s and later wrote down. Moreover, Bournonville also included a number of Jules Perrot's striking male variations, invented by that fellow student of his during the years of his Parisian sojourn (1826–29).

The 'Dancing School' thus represents one of the most profound insights into the development of French ballet technique in the 1820s to survive into our time, upon which Bournonville based and later developed his own style and dance technique.

The photographs available for *Conservatoriet* date almost exclusively from the first decades of the present century. Though rather few in number, they testify to the particular French vaudeville charm that has continued to ensure this ballet's popularity.

176 (1912). Act I: '. . . A *salle de danse* with almost no furniture. Doors to the sides and in the middle . . .'

177 (1909). Christian Christensen as Dufour (26.12.1897); Act I, scene 1:
'. . . Dufour [the *Inspecteur* at the Conservatoire], in dishabille, enters, deeply engrossed in reading a newspaper . . . He is pursued by his housekeeper [Mamsel Bonjour], who showers him with reproaches to which he does not seem to pay any attention . . .'

178 (1909). (cont.) '. . . he has advertised himself as an anonymous suitor. Dufour, who wishes to give up his bachelor status, flatters himself with the thought that his personal merits will secure him a favourable match . . .'

179 (c. 1912). Hans Beck as Alexis (21.3.1886); Act I, scene 4:
'. . . The signal is given for the class to begin, and with the utmost seriousness the dancers all commence their exercises, which are led in turn by Alexis and the female soloists . . .'

180 (1879). Anna Tychsen as Eliza (6.3.1879); Act I, scene 4:
'. . . *Pas d'école* with variations . . .'

181 (1933). Poul Witzansky as Raimbaud, the old fiddler (3.12.1933), Else Højgaard as Eliza (3.12.1933), Margot Lander as Victorine (3.12.1933) and corps de ballet; Act I, scene 4:
'. . . *Pas d'école* with variations . . .'

183 (1909). Christian Christensen as Dufour (26.12.1897); Act I, scene 5:
'. . . Dufour enters, trying to finish his dressing [for his rural rendezvous] as quickly as possible . . .'

182 (1933). Margot Lander as Victorine (3.12.1933), Leif Ørnberg as Erneste (3.12.1933), Else Højgaard as Eliza (3.12.1933), Børge Ralov as Alexis (3.12.1933); Act I, scene 4:
'. . . The class is over. The ladies take a rest. Erneste [a young violinist] tells them of an amusing matrimonial advertisement . . . it is none other than M. Dufour who intends to enter the state of matrimony in this adventurous way . . . The young people are struck with the idea of playing a trick on the vain Dufour in order to avenge the deceived spinster [Mamsel Bonjour]. They decide to put in an appearance at the site of his rural rendezvous . . .'

184 (1912). Act II: '. . . The restaurant of the Pavillon Henri IV on the terrace at St-Germain. On all sides, tables and garden chairs, boskquets and flower beds. In the background is revealed the glorious prospect across the valley of the Seine to Paris . . .'

185 (1912). Karl Merrild as Jules, a student (1.12.1912); Act II, scene 1:
'. . . A merry crowd of students and grisettes returns [to the restaurant] from strolling and fishing . . . riding crops are handed out and, pawing and prancing, they perform a contredanse that, in its gaiety, is reminiscent of Chaumière's balls and Mussard's masquerades . . .'

186 (c. 1898). Ellen Price as Eliza (13.9.1898); Act II, scene 3:
'. . . The waiter announces a veiled lady. There now follows a scene of "advances", sentimentality, and roguishness. Dufour tries in vain to persuade the lady to lift her veil. This results in a graceful allemande, in which everyone, with the exception of Dufour, recognises the piquant Eliza . . .'

187 (1909). Christian Christensen as Dufour (26.12.1897); Act II, scene 4:
'. . . She allows him to kiss her hand, promises to return and exits. The captivated Dufour is gazing after the departing beauty . . .'

188 (1912). Grethe Ditlevsen as Victorine, disguised as an English lady (1.12.1912); Act II, scene 5:
'. . . A lady dressed somewhat according to English fashion approaches . . .'

189 (c. 1861). Petrine Fredstrup as Victorine, disguised as an English lady (15.9.1850); Act II, scene 5:
'. . . She sits down, peers at Dufour through her lorgnette, and asks if it is he who made the proposal of marriage in the newspaper . . .'

190 (1933). Harry Larsen as Dufour (3.12.1933) and Else Højgaard as Victorine (3.12.1933); Act II, scene 5: '. . . [Dufour] seems to please this lady. She praises his physique and declares that he must dance the Polka superbly. Dufour, who has never in his life danced the Polka, allows himself to be carried away by the damsel's flattery and hops about as best as he can . . .'

191 (1933). Else Højgaard as Eliza (3.12.1933), Kirsten Gnatt as Fanny, a poor dance student whose admittance to the Conservatoire earlier has been refused by Dufour (3.12.1933), Margot Lander as Victorine (3.12.1933); Act II, scene 8:
'. . . Guests flock to the restaurant . . . Three graceful sylphides [Eliza, Fanny and Victorine] glide into the circle. The garden of the Pavillon is transformed into a stage, the tables and chairs into a gallery and a parterre. The trio is greeted with thunderous applause and admiration for art is blended with acknowledgement of nobility of soul . . .'

192 (1933). Else Højgaard as Eliza (3.12.1933), Kirsten Gnatt as Fanny (3.12.1933), Margot Lander as Victorine (3.12.1933), Tony Madsen as Jeanne, Fanny's mother (3.12.1933), Poul Witzansky as Raimbaud (3.12.1933), Harry Larsen as Dufour (3.12.1933), Ragnhild Rasmussen as Mamsel Bonjour (3.12.1933), two unidentified children; Act II, scene 8:
'. . . The tambourine is passed around and filled to the brim with coins and bank notes. The poor [Raimbaud] family is aided [by Dufour, who is forced to acknowledge Fanny's talent] and Fanny is adopted by the pretty *danseuses*, who promise to guide her along the pathway of art . . .'

The Kermesse in Brüges, or The Three Gifts

Romantic Ballet in 3 Acts.
Music by Holger Simon Paulli.
Scenery by Christian Ferdinand Christensen.
Costumes by Edvard Lehmann.
Premiered on April 4, 1851.
Still in repertory.
Number of performances by June 1986: 284.

Although Bournonville never visited the Low Countries, he set one of his most charming and fanciful 'travelogues' in that environment.

According to his memoirs, he found the inspiration for *The Kermesse in Brüges* in the Flemish painter Gerard Dou's many genre pictures of Flemish burghers, and in particular the 1663 painting 'A Violin-player at the Window' (today in the Dresden Gallery). Dou's genre pictures, including this painting, were most popular in the last century, being extensively reproduced as copperplate engravings. Obviously the painting provided Bournonville with a clear motif, from which he created a story about the fantastic adventures of the three brothers, Adrian, Geert, and Carelis, of whom the latter is given a magic violin by the old alchemist Mirewelt, as a sign of gratitude for having saved his life in a murderous hold-up.

The fantastic plot provided Bournonville with the opportunity for a great number of grotesque and burlesque situations as well as a large number of dance divertissements, which all together secured the ballet's fortune.

More dances, however, were soon added to the ballet. The popular *Slovanka* (originally part of the shortlived 1857 ballet *In the Carpathians*) was thus incorporated in Act I in 1865 (see note for no. 194), while the Act II pas de deux divertissement performed at Van Everdingen's was incorporated in 1909, being transferred from Auber's opera *La Muette de Portici*, for which it had originally been choreographed in 1873 (see introduction for that opera).

At the ballet's premiere, a critic praised Bournonville's ability to create a true illusion of seventeenth-century Flemish street life, but found the plot itself much inferior to those of his previous 'travelogues' such as *The Toreador* and *Napoli*, saying: 'It looks as if [Bournonville's] talent to create picturesque scenes is at the same time his strength and weakness, since most of his supreme picturesque situations seem to block a true dramatic flow.' (*Fædrelandet*, April 5, 1851).

The photographs for *Kermesse in Brüges*, which cover some fifty years of performance, centre on two larger series (here only presented in selection), taken by Peter Elfelt (1905 & 1909) and featuring Ellen Price de Plane as Mirewelt's daughter, Eleonore, with Gustav Uhlendorff as Carelis, performing their charming love duets in Acts I and II. The photographs also testify to the subtle but significant changes in the costumes that took place over these fifty years, such as can be seen for instance by comparing nos. 195 and 196, and nos. 208 and 209.

193 (1900). Act I (& Act III):
'. . . A marketplace in Bruges, decorated as if for a fair. To the right, [the alchemist] Mirewelt's house; to the left, upstage, a tavern . . .'

63

194 (1910). Aage Eibye, Karl Merrild and Kaj Smith as three Hungarians (7.11.1909); Act I, *Slovanka*:
'. . . Popular rejoicing with processions, drinking bouts and dancing [a *Slovanka* performed by three couples of Gipsy girls and Hungarian boys], and merriment . . .'

195 (1884). Anna Tychsen as Eleonore (8.12.1872), Act I:
'. . . Mirewelt, with his daughter [Eleonore], is sitting outside his house. Carelis asks Eleonore [with a flower] to dance . . .'

196 (1905). Gustav Uhlendorff as Carelis (9.9.1900) and Ellen Price de Plane as Eleonore (9.9.1900); Act I, *Pas de deux*:
'. . . and the young couple delight everyone with their grace and lightness . . .'

197 (1905). (cont.) '. . . Mirewelt learns that the brothers [Adrian, Geert and Carelis] are about to sally forth into the wide world, and he wishes to give each of them a gift to take with him . . . the lighthearted Carelis obtains a *viola da gamba* which will impel everyone to dance . . .'

198 (1900). Act II, first set: '. . . Mirewelt's study. To the left, a large fireplace and the entrance to the other rooms in the house; to the right, an exit. Upstage [here situated at downstage left] a window . . .'

199 (1909). Ellen Price de Plane as Eleonore (9.9.1900); Act II, first set:
'. . . Eleonore wakens by her father's couch [and contemplates the rose given to her by Carelis] . . .'

200 (1900). Act II, first set, Tableau:
.'. . . There is a knocking at the door. Marchen and Johanna, who are worried about their lovers [Adrian and Geert], wish to consult the wise men, and Mirewelt reads their horoscopes. They see, in turn, Adrian surrounded by perils of war . . .'

201 (1900). (cont.) Tableau '. . . and Geert revelling in a sybaritic existence . . .'

202 (1909). Ellen Price de Plane as Eleonore (9.9.1900); Act II, first set:
'. . . The sisters' despair vents itself in tears [while Eleonore prays that nothing ill shall happen to Carelis on his way out in the wide world] . . .'

203 (1909). (cont.) '. . . suddenly they hear a melody which makes them dance in spite of themselves . . .'

204 (c. 1865). Harald Scharff as Carelis (19.11.1865); Act II, first set:
'. . . It is Carelis [appearing in the window], who consoles them with the fact that his brothers still love them and will soon return . . .'

205 (1909). Ellen Price de Plane as Eleonore (9.9.1900) and Gustav Uhlendorff as Carelis (9.9.1900); Act II, first set:
'. . . Carelis is left alone with Eleonore . . . His expressions soon become more tender, and she wishes to leave; but he lures her back, dancing to the magical power of the sounds . . .'

206 (1900). Act II, second set: '. . . The stage is transformed into a magnificent garden in the old-fashioned style. In the background, the Castle of Everdingen and a terrace looking out over the water . . .'

207 (1909). Christian Christensen as Claës (27.8.1891); Act II, second set: '. . . The butler calls Geert over into a corner to inform him that a veiled lady [who has dropped her handkerchief] wishes to speak with him . . .'

208 (c. 1861). Petrine Fredstrup as Marchen (4.4.1851); Act II, second set: '. . . But what can equal Geert's horror and astonishment when he recognises his deserted fiancée. Marchen showers him with anger and reproaches . . .'

209 (c. 1891). Olga Uhlendorff as Marchen (27.8.1891); Act II, second set: '... [Marchen's] mother and Johanna appear and try to effect a reconciliation. They finally succeed. Geert repents his errors, embraces his beloved Marchen, and as a proof that he will never again be unfaithful to her, he gives her the magic ring...'

210 (c. 1909). Ellen Tegner as Johanna (9.9.1900); Act II, second set: '... [because of the cavaliers' undivided attention to Marchen] Geert begins to suspect the power of the ring, takes it from Marchen's finger, and gives it to Johanna, who immediately becomes the object of the gentlemen's admiration...'

211 (1909). Gustav Uhlendorff as Carelis (9.9.1900); Act III, second set: '... The condemned [Mirewelt, Adrian and Geert] are brought forth ... while the executioners set up the stake ... [Dejectedly Carelis] seizes his viola da gamba and with a couple of rapid strokes [of the bow] transforms the whole atmosphere...'

212 (1909). Christian Christensen as a Flemish Burgher (27.8.1891); Act III, second set: '... Judges, executioners, ladies, gentlemen, old women, soldiers and children romp around in the wildest dance. Never has any Kermesse seen such a dance. Everyone dances, leaps, and swings...'

The Wedding Festival in Hardanger

Ballet in 2 Acts.
Music by Holger Simon Paulli.
Scenery by Christian Ferdinand Christensen (Act I, second set) and Troels Lund (Act I, first set & Act II).
Costumes by Edvard Lehmann.
Premiered on March 4, 1853.
Last performance: May 10, 1929 (a freely adapted version with choreography by Flemming Flindt to a score arranged by Egil Monn Iversen was produced by the Norwegian National Ballet (*Den Norske Opera*), Oslo, and premiered on March 26, 1982).
Number of performances by 1929: 173.

Throughout his life Bournonville was a true admirer of the majestic nature and the rich national customs of Norway, which he encountered as a tourist as well as on professional tours in the summers of 1840 and 1852.

Resting from a number of successful performances in that country in 1852, he spent a few days at an inn at the farmstead of Jonsrud (in the valley of the river Lomme south-east of Oslo), where he had the opportunity to see a number of local dances performed by a young peasant named Jørgen, claimed to be the most skilful dancer of the entire district. His performance of the local versions of *Springdans* and *Halling* was an experience which Bournonville later described thus: 'Norwegian dances, which in all their simplicity contained material enough for me to compose endless variations . . . I reaped great profit from Jørgen's worthy presentations.'

In 1852 Bournonville was further spurred to create a two-act ballet on Norwegian themes, having studied the famous 1848 painting by Norwegian artists Adolph Tidemand and Hans Gude 'A Wedding in Hardanger' – already staged as a *tableau vivant* in Christiania (now Oslo) in 1849 by the painters themselves – as well as a number of other works by leading Norwegian painters, whose mastery was recognised by Bournonville in his comment: 'The deep feeling that is expressed through their compositions transforms the delightful paintings into moving poems.'

Moreover, two tales by Norwegian writers Andreas Faye (*Norske Sagn*, 1833), and Nicolai Ramm Østgaard (the novel *To Fæsterpiger*, 1852) provided him with material enough for a two-act ballet, the action of which was divided between two very different pairs of lovers (Ragnhild and Halvor set against Kirsti and Ola) and which reached a dramatic climax at the end of Act I. Against it, Act II was entirely dedicated to picturing the joyous and festive atmosphere of a Norwegian peasant wedding in a rich succession of national dances and popular customs, which together secured the long lasting success of the ballet. In quoting Bournonville's own preface, in which he characterises the ballet as 'an art work of a more pictorial than dramatic nature', the critic of *Berlingske Tidende* (March 5, 1853) accepted the rather thin plot of Act I and praised the 'genious talent' with which Bournonville in Act II produced a picture – albeit hardly typical – of the many peculiar customs that take place during a Norwegian wedding.

However, on the first production of the ballet after Bournonville's death, the critic of *Dagbladet* (January 23, 1880) stressed the lack of dramatic continuity between the two acts, finding it rather strange that the bridal couple of Act II were not given any connection whatsoever with the dramatic action of the ballet's first act.

In spite of these 'errors of construction', the ballet became one of Bournonville's most popular works, and achieved the highest number of performances of all of his ballets during his own lifetime.

213 (1903?). Act I, scenes 1–5 (& Act II, scenes 1–2): '. . . A log room with beam ceiling at the farmstead of "Vold". Through the open door upstage a mountain landscape can be seen. To the right and left, doors leading to the other rooms in the house . . .'

214 (1911). Grethe Ditlevsen as Ragnhild (never performed on stage) and Gustav Uhlendorff as Halvor (6.5.1903); Act I, scene 1:
'. . . Guri is dozing at her spinning wheel. Her daughter, Ragnhild, is holding a book, a passage of which she has read, but her thoughts are elsewhere. Vibrating tones are heard; it is a jews-harp . . .'

215 (1905). Gustav Uhlendorff as Halvor (6.5.1903) and Ellen Price de Plane as Ragnhild (1.2.1905); Act I, scene 1:
'. . . She recognises the melody and perceives Halvor, who enters with noise-less tread . . .'

216 (1905). (cont.) '. . . for they must not awaken the mother . . .'

217 (1911). Grethe Ditlevsen as Ragnhild (never performed on stage) and Gustav Uhlendorff as Halvor (6.5.1903); Act I, scene 1:
'. . . The lovers cautiously greet one another . . . They have so much to say to each other, but are at loss for words . . .'

70

218 (1905). Gustav Uhlendorff as Halvor (6.5.1903) and Ellen Price de Plane as Ragnhild (1.2.1905); Act I, scene 1:
'. . . and the quivering but familiar sounds [of the jews-harp] must express their feelings . . .'

219 (1911). Gustav Uhlendorff as Halvor (6.5.1903), Grethe Ditlevsen as Ragnhild (never performed on stage) and Richard Jensen as Ola (15.9.1916); Act I, scene 2:
'. . . Arne [Ragnhild's father] comes from the woods, deep in intimate conversation with Ola [Ragnhild's rich suitor]. He bids him enter, but they are taken aback at the sight of the lovers . . .'

220 (1911). (cont.) '. . . Ola swaggers over to Halvor to show him his silver buttons and brooch, his pipe mountings, and his full wallet . . .'

221 (1907). Hans Beck as Ola (6.5.1902); Act I, scene 2:
'. . . he presents a magnificent prayer book as a betrothal gift to Ragnhild . . .'

71

222 (1911). Grethe Ditlevsen as Ragnhild (never performed on stage) and Richard Jensen as Ola (15.9.1916); Act I, scene 2:
'. . . who is sitting in a corner brokenhearted and aggrieved [being denied her union with Halvor] . . .'

223 (1903). Christian Christensen as The Bridegroom (9.11.1887); Act I, scene 3:
'. . . a visitor has arrived. It is the bridegroom from the farmstead of "Heja" who has come to invite them to a wedding . . .'

224 (1903 ?). Act I, second set, scenes 6–10:
'. . . The mountainous region at Hardanger Fjord. On both sides, pine and birch woods. To the right, an old bell tower, and, behind it, a path leading up to the church, which cannot be seen. Some large stones are lying on the shore . . .'

225 (1881). Marie Westberg as Kirsti (21.1.1880); Act I, scene 6:
'. . . Peasants of various ages have flocked to this spot to view the wedding procession, which is expected to arrive here by water. They meet Kirsti, the young sæter girl, and greet her in friendly fashion. But she diffidently avoids them . . .'

226 (1903). Ellen Braunstein as Kirsti (6.5.1903); Act I, scene 6:
'. . . when the maids hand her a nosegay with which to greet the bridal party, she tears it to pieces . . .'

227 (c. 1861). Petrine Fredstrup as Kirsti (13.5.1859); Act I, scene 6:
'. . . scatters the flowers at her feet, and indicates that thus have her youth and happiness been wasted. All regard her with sadness and sympathy . . .'

228 (c. 1880–84). Athalia Flammé as The Bride (21.1.1880) and Hans Beck as The Bridegroom (21.1.1880); Act I, scene 7:
'. . . Three decorated boats put in at the landingplace . . . the third bears the bridal couple . . .'

229 (1903). Christian Christensen as The Bridegroom (9.11.1887) and Clara Rasmussen as The Bride (6.5.1903); Act I, scene 7:
'. . . They are greeted with jubilation. The musicians strike up a solemn march . . . The bride, with a golden crown on her head, is congratulated while she loyally shakes the bridegroom's hand . . .'

230 (1911). Emilie Smith as Kirsti (15.9.1916) and Richard Jensen as Ola (15.9.1916); Act I, scene 8:
'. . . Kirsti . . . fearfully draws near to speak with Ola. The latter is not happy to see her . . . there was once a more tender relationship between them, but the faithless lover's embarrassment is expressed by scorn rather than regret . . .'

231 (1929). Elna Jørgen-Jensen as Kirsti (4.5.1929), Richard Jensen as Ola (4.5.1929) and Leif Ørnberg as Halvor (4.5.1929); Act I, scene 8:
'. . . and when Halvor happens to enter just then, Ola even goes so far as to propose that he and Kirsti become a couple . . .'

232 (1911). Emilie Smith as Kirsti (15.9.1916), Richard Jensen as Ola (15.9.1916) Gustav Uhlendorff as Halvor (6.5.1903), Grethe Ditlevsen as Ragnhild (never performed on stage); Act I, scene 8: '. . . Their indignation only increases his hilarity . . . and, in his half-drunken state . . . he tumbles backward into the water. Kirsti and Halvor stand there, petrified with fright . . .'

74

233 (1911). (cont.) '. . . Kirsti hastens to the tower to ring the alarm bell. [scene 9:] Everybody comes running, dismayed at this unlucky omen on a wedding day. But Halvor has brought his rival up from the depths and, with the aid of some other young men, brings him ashore, half dead . . .'

234 (1911). (cont.) '. . . Ola gradually regains consciousness. He stares about him in bewilderment, and his gaze comes to rest upon his saviour. Shamefaced and bowed down, he goes over to Halvor, shakes hands with him . . . and indicates that Halvor is . . . the only man worthy of Ragnhild . . .'

235 (1884). Charlotte Hansen as The Bride wearing the married woman's hat (21.2.1884); Act I, scene 10:
'. . . The wedding party prepares to set sail . . . the boat [with the newly married couple] glides toward the fjord . . .'

236 (1881). Marie Westberg as Kirsti (21.1.1880); Act I, scene 10:
'. . . On a stone near the church sits the deeply shaken and remorseful Ola. A consolatory spirit approaches him; it is his cast-off sweetheart. He sees her, takes her hand, offers her the prayer book . . .'

237 (1911). Richard Jensen as Ola (15.9.1916) and Emilie Smith as Kirsti (15.9.1916); Act I, scene 10:
'. . . and all is well again [between the two] . . .'

238 (1905). Ellen Price de Plane as Ragnhild (1.2.1905) and Gustav Uhlendorff as Halvor (6.5.1903); Act II, scene 1 (scenery as no. 213):
'. . . [Ragnhild] hears rapid footsteps. The sound draws nearer, and Halvor, out of breath, comes bursting through the door. He has run all the way to bring the glad tidings [that their union has been approved] . . .'

239 (c. 1891–95). Valborg Jørgensen as Ragnhild, in festal dress (15.4.1891); Act II, scene 2: '. . . Ola and his fiancée [Kirsti] appear just in time to corroborate Halvor's statements . . . Delighted with her bold and faithful lover Ragnhild gives him her hand and promises to go with him to the wedding . . . Kirsti helps her to don her festal dress . . .'

240 (1911). Richard Jensen as Ola (15.9.1916), Emilie Smith as Kirsti (15.9.1916), Gustav Uhlendorff as Halvor (6.5.1903), Grethe Ditlevsen as Ragnhild (never performed on stage); Act II, scene 2, *Halling Dance*:
'. . . and amid dancing and merry jumps, the two happy couples hasten off to the celebration [at the farmstead of "Heja"] . . .'

241 (1903?). Act II, scenes 3–4: '. . . The parlour at the farmstead of "Heja", decorated as for a wedding . . .'

242 (1903). Clara Rasmussen as The Bride (6.5.1903) and Christian Christensen as The Bridegroom (9.11.1887); Act II, scene 3:
'. . . The meal is over, the fiddlers begin to play, and the floor is cleared for dancing. First the bride and groom dance with each other . . .'

243 (1903). (cont.) *The Bridal Dance*.

244 (1929). Centre group: Ragnhild Rasmussen as The Bridegroom's mother (4.5.1929), Margot Florentz-Gerhard as The Bride (4.5.1929), Tony Madsen as The Bride's mother (4.5.1929), Laura Herreborg as Guri (4.5.1929); (to the far left) Kirsten Nellemose as Ragnhild (4.5.1929); (to the far right) Elna Jørgen-Jensen as Kirsti (4.5.1929) and corps de ballet; Act II, scene 4:
'. . . The most important moment of the celebration draws nigh. The golden crown is to be taken from the bride's head and she herself must designate the one who shall be next to wear it. She chooses Ragnhild . . .'

245 (1920). Svend Aage Larsen (1.6.1920), Holger Mehnen (1.6.1920), Svend Carlo Jensen (1.6.1920); Act II, scene 3, *The Barber Dance*:
'. . . Three young fellows perform a comic scene which, under the name "The Barber Dance", furnishes the opportunity for several characteristic episodes . . .'

246 (1903). Clara Rasmussen as The Bride (6.5.1903) and Christian Christensen as The Bridegroom (9.11.1897); Act II, scene 4:
'. . . the bridegroom must undergo one more test . . . he must seek out and capture his [hiding] wife . . . With a mischievous expression she presents him with the red "pixie hat", which is the hallmark of his new estate . . .'

247 (1929). Margot Florentz-Gerhard as The Bride (4.5.1929) and Gunnar Iversen as The Bridegroom (4.5.1929); Act II, scene 4, *Halling Dance*:
'. . . Now begins the *Halling*, wherein the young husband performs his daring kicks at the rafters with the bright hat on his head . . .'

248 (1929). Leif Ørnberg as Halvor (4.5.1929) and Kirsten Nellemose as Ragnhild (4.5.1929); Act II, scene 4, *Spring Dance*:
'. . . The guests applaud, and it is Halvor and Ragnhild who lead the *springdans* . . .'

249 (1904). Richard Jensen and Agnes Nyrop as guests at the wedding at 'Heja' (6.5.1903); Act II, scene 4, *Spring Dance*:
'. . . Everyone, young and old alike, takes part in it. Joy has reached its height, and on jubilant groups the curtain falls . . .'

A Folk Tale

Ballet in 3 Acts.
Music composed by Niels W. Gade (Acts I & III) and Iohan Peter Emilius Hartmann (Act II).
Scenery by Christian Ferdinand Christensen (Acts I & III) and Troels Lund (Act II).
Costumes by Edvard Lehmann.
Premiered on March 20, 1854.
Still in repertory.
Number of performances by June 1986: 429.

'The most complete and best of all my choreographic works'.

Thus was *A Folk Tale* characterised by Bournonville in his memoirs in 1865 – eleven years after the ballet's creation, and at a time when he was still in the midst of exploring the possibilities of the choreographic art with such massive ballet visions as his works on Northern mythology *The Valkyrie* (1861), and the later *The Lay of Thrym* (1868). *A Folk Tale* was certainly unique, not only to Bournonville but as well to his contemporaries and imminent successors. Already at the premiere a critic was impressed by the ballet's innate 'national values', while forty years later, in Hans Beck's 1894 production, it even became ranked with 'the Nation's true and imperishable stage relics'. Since then *A Folk Tale* has been among the most popular and often performed Bournonville ballets.

Although claiming in his memoirs that the main inspiration for this ballet was found in the four-volume collection of Danish folk tales collected and published by writer Just Mathias Thiele 1818–23, Bournonville must also have found some balletic inspiration in Friedrich Kuhlau's tremendously successful score of Danish folk tunes arranged for Johan Ludvig Heiberg's 1828 national fairy play *The Elves' Hill*. An even stronger and more specific balletic influence might have come from Joseph Mazilier's 1839 ballet *La Gipsy*, which Bournonville saw performed at the Paris Opéra in the spring of 1841, and from the plot of which a great number of elements can be traced in *A Folk Tale*. With the story of *A Folk Tale* leading to a harmonious happy ending, however, it differs essentially in both spirit and style from *La Gipsy*, which ends in true French-style romantic tragedy.

A Folk Tale's strong accent on the victory of Christianity over the subterranean diabolic forces was, moreover, musically supported by a score of hitherto unknown beauty and finish, personally commissioned by Bournonville from two of Denmark's most eminent composers of the time, Niels W. Gade and Iohan Peter Emilius Hartmann. With his music for Acts I and III, Gade initiates a new era in Danish ballet music. The traditional dance music structures now gave way to a free and more ballade-like music idiom within a new and more specific Danish folk tone sonority. The dances in *A Folk Tale* are thus all characterised by a strong rhythmical conciseness and refined pastoral sonority, which made Gade the composer who could best release the weightless floating and inner poetry of Bournonville's choreography. Moreover, *A Folk Tale* represents some of the finest musical interaction ever between the delicate national lyricism of Gade and the characteristic Nordic-romantic sonority of Hartmann.

With Hartmann's burlesque and bewitched music for the subterranean second act, the ballet came to represent the beginning of the most fruitful and enduring collaboration Bournonville was ever to have with a composer.

In European ballet history only few ballets can thus be claimed to reflect, in music as well as in choreography, the spirit and character of an entire nation so fully as does *A Folk Tale*. Mainly for that reason the ballet belongs among those of Bournonville's works that have been best preserved, having undergone only one major revision by Hans Beck in 1894, when the infectious *Elf maiden's dance* of Act I was extended to be performed by thirty-two maidens instead of the original twelve, to make better use of the larger stage of the new Royal Theatre. Moreover, Beck added twelve women to take part in the *Troll's dance* of Act II, which up to that time had been performed exclusively by men, since it was considered of too bad taste, in Bournonville's own time, to have women taking part in these 'wild and ugly dances'.

The photographs selected here cover a period of nearly seventy years of performance. They reflect in particular some of the period's stylistic changes in depicting Danish Renaissance by means of scenery and costumes, such as for instance the dress of Frøken Birthe (nos. 251 and 252), or the *Pas de sept* (nos. 279 and 280) to name only a few.

250 (1908). Act I, scenes 1–2: '. . . A piece of woodland at the foot of a hill covered with scrub . . .'

80

251 (c. 1861). Petrine Fredstrup as Frøken Birthe (20.3.1854); Act I, scene 1: '... The people of the manor are busy laying a table beneath an old oak tree. Hunting horns are heard nearby. It is the unpredictable Frøken Birthe, who has ordered the repast to be served at this spot ...'

252 (1907). Ellen Tegner as Frøken Birthe (3.12.1902); Act I, scene 2: '... The Frøken proposes several dances and games in which she displays her bizarre humour ...'

253 (1922). Act I, scene 3: '... Darkness falls ... Despite the warnings, the Junker stays behind in the forest and, brooding, sits down near the hill ...'

254 (1894). Valborg Jørgensen as Hilda (29.4.1894); Act I, scene 3:
'. . . Subterranean music is heard, and the hill rises on four flaming pillars: [in the midst] stands a lovely maiden in dazzling raiment with a golden cup in her hand. With gliding steps she approaches Junker Ove and gives him the brimming cup . . .'

255 (c. 1870). Waldemar Price as Junker Ove (13.2.1864); Act I, scene 3:
'. . . He takes it with his gaze immoveably fixed on the ethereal being, but pours its contents onto the ground, whereupon bluish flames spout from the grass . . .'

256 (1913). Carl Hillebrandt as Junker Ove (9.11.1913), Ludvig Brandstrup as Diderik (9.11.1913), Ellen Price de Plane as Hilda (10.5.1908), Victoria Petersen as Muri (9.11.1913), Georg Christensen as Viderik (9.11.1913); Act I, scene 3:
'. . . The Mountain Lass demands that he return the cup; she threatens and entices. But Ove is determined to keep it . . .'

257 (1929). Kaj Smith as Junker Ove (1.9.1929) and Gertrud Jensen as Hilda (1.9.1929); Act I, scene 3:
'. . . there now ensues a struggle during which the Troll Woman finally loses patience and drags the maiden back inside, while giving a sign for the hill to close . . .'

258 (c. 1895). Waldemar Price as Junker Ove (13.2.1864) and the elf maidens; Act I, scene 3:
'. . . [The Troll Woman calls] forth the elf maidens from the depths of the swamp. In flowing garments, with rushes and water lilies in their unbound hair, they encircle Ove and sweep him along in their whirling dance . . .'

259 (1922). Act II, scenes 1–2 & 4: '. . . The Troll Woman's [Muri's] subterranean hall. Centre stage [here to the right], a large hearth with forges on both sides . . .'
Scene 3, Hilda's dream:
'. . . A nurse sits rocking a tiny child. Next to her stands a table with a lamp and a golden cup. A group of angels, kneeling before the symbol of the cross, passes the cradle and the sleeping nurse . . .'

260 (c. 1884–88). Laura Frederiksen as Muri (28.4.1857); Act II, scene 1:
'. . . Muri is standing at the hearth [with the distaff which she hands over to Hilda before] making pancakes . . .'

261 (1894). Valborg Jørgensen as Hilda (29.4.1894); Act II, scene 1:
'. . . Hilda [dances while] spinning on her distaff . . .'

262 (c. 1903). Christian Christensen as Diderik (29.4.1894); Act II, scene 2:
'. . . Diderik's proposal [to Hilda], which essentially consists in bedecking his beloved with all the jewellery he and his brother [Viderik] have made for her, is not successful . . . His transitions from flattery to indignation only serve to emphasise his ugliness . . .'

263 (1894). Valborg Jørgensen as Hilda (29.4.1894); Act II, scene 2:
'. . . Hilda [bedecked with Diderik's jewellery] gives him to understand that while she may be very fond of him, she will on no account have him for a husband . . . she dances rollickingly about him . . .'

264 (c. 1867–76). Frederik Ferdinand Hoppensach as Diderik (20.3.1854); Act II, scene 2:
'. . . [Diderik] runs off threateningly to complain to his mother . . .'

265 (1894). Valborg Jørgensen as Hilda (29.4.1894); Act II, scene 3:
'. . . Hilda awakens [from her dream (see no. 259)]. Everything has vanished. She strives in vain to recollect her dream. She remembers only one thing clearly, and, finding two sticks near the hearth, she fashions them into a Cross . . .'

266 (c. 1867). Betty Schnell as Hilda (20.9.1867); Act II, scene 3:
'. . . She kneels before it as did the angel in the cloud . . .'

267 (1916). Elna Jørgen-Jensen as Hilda (13.6.1916) and Holger Strøm as Viderik (13.6.1916); Act II, scene 4:
'. . . Hilda arranges to flee with Viderik when the troll dance [at the wedding party] is at its wildest. They carry out their plan and disappear through the forge . . .'

268 (1922). Act III, scenes 1–3:
'. . . The outskirts of a forest. To the left, a well with a picture of St John. In the background, fields and meadows; farther off, the manor house, and in the distance, the heath . . .'

269 (1894). Valborg Jørgensen as Hilda (29.4.1894); Act III, scene 1:
'. . . Hilda, in rustic dress, emerges [with Viderik] from the thicket. The dwarf is amused at the old people's superstition [about the well's healing water], but Hilda . . . is kind to the poor [and distributes her jewellery among the invalids] . . .'

270 (c. 1881–99). Waldemar Price as Junker Ove (13.2.1864); Act III, scene 2:
'. . . Junker Ove approaches. His whole manner bears the stamp of quiet madness; everywhere he thinks he sees the elf maidens' dance . . . The peasants sympathetically move out of his way. Only Hilda remains . . . to ask about the cup, which he is still holding in his hand . . .'

271 (1908). Act III, scene 4: '. . . Frøken Birthe's chamber in the manor house . . .'

272 (c. 1870). Laura Stillmann as Else, a kitchen maid (20.3.1854); Act III, scene 4: '. . . As Dorte [Frøken Birthe's maid] is standing in front of the mirror [trying the Frøken's clothes on] the pantry maid [Else] enters with the Frøken's drink. She too wants to deck herself out . . . and soon the whole wardrobe has been apportioned . . .'

273 (c. 1861). Petrine Fredstrup as Frøken Birthe (20.3.1854); Act III, scene 4: '. . . A bell sounds . . . Birthe, in a dressing gown, enters and displays all her bad humour during her more than difficult toilette . . . The maids, who are now driven to extremes, rebel. The Frøken cries for help but is overcome by her vehemence and has a fit . . .'

274 (c.1870). Betty Schnell as Hilda (20.9.1867); Act III, scene 4:
'. . . At this moment, Hilda comes flying into the room . . . this place seems to remind her of her dream and the lovely cradle song. She sees the old nurse, slowly leads her over to the armchair and places herself in her lap . . .'

275 (1907). Ellen Tegner as Frøken Birthe (3.12.1902); Act III, scene 4:
'. . . Birthe awakens from her swoon and again becomes enraged at the sight of the homage being paid to this strange girl. She orders them to chase Hilda away. But instead of obeying her, they try to exorcise her, for she must be a troll . . .'

276 (1922). Act III, scenes 5–6 and final score: [seperate set since September 24, 1922] '. . . The wood near the well . . .'

277 (c. 1896). Anna Harboe as FrøkenBirthe (22.3.1896); Act III, scene 6:
'. . . Frøken Birthe comes rushing in to ask for help against her rebellious servants.
She discovers Viderik, who freely and familiarly approaches Birthe . . . her sudden
outburst of ill temper, her clenched fists and her stamping feet clearly confirm that
Birthe is a *troll* . . .'

278 (1868). Betty Schnell as Hilda (20.9.1867); Act III, final score:
'. . . Hilda, richly dressed [for her wedding with Junker Ove] and surrounded by
distinguished kinsmen, enters and receives the homage of all . . .'

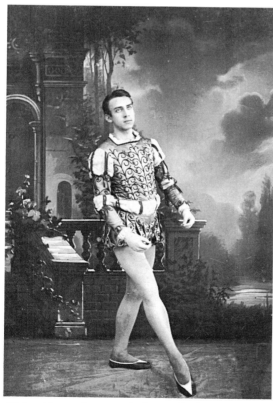

279 (c. 1903). Richard Jensen (1.12.1903); Act III, final score, *Pas de sept*:
'. . . Music sounds, dancing heightens the joy, and beneath the decorated Maypole,
Midsummer is celebrated . . .'

280 (1922). Karl Merrild (10.1.1912); Act III, final score, *Pas de sept*.

La Ventana

Divertissement in 2 Scenes.

Music by Hans Christian Lumbye (Scene I) and Vilhelm Christian Holm (Scene II).

Scenery arranged by Christian Ferdinand Christensen.

Costumes by Edvard Lehmann.

Premiered on October 6, 1856 (Final Version).

Still in repertory.

Number of performances by June 1986 (including Court Theatre, 1854): 382.

La Ventana was originally a single mirror dance, created for and premiered by the sisters Juliette and Sophie Price in a charity performance given by the Price family at Copenhagen's Court Theatre on June 19, 1854.

This mirror dance – a popular motif in the Romantic Ballet – at once became immensely popular with the audience, and was included in the repertory of the Royal Theatre on December 26 the same year.

Returning to Copenhagen from his engagement as ballet-master in Vienna for the 1855–56 season, Bournonville remounted *La Ventana* on October 6, 1856, in an extended version with a new outdoor second scene. This scene included a newly choreographed pas de trois divertissement followed by a final *Seguidilla*, the latter being partially based on a popular *Seguidilla*, choreographed by Paul Taglioni and performed as the Finale of Joseph Mazilier's ballet *Die Verwandelten Weiber* (*Le Diable à quatre*) at Vienna's Kärtnerthore Theatre on October 30, 1855.

Bournonville was not blind to the romantic qualities to be found in the Spanish national dances, but at the same time he deeply detested what he called 'the flood of lascivious Spanish *bailadores*', who appeared on nearly all European stages in the 1840s and '50s as a result of the immense popularity of the Spanish dances following Fanny Elssler's sensational triumphs with *La Cachucha* at the Paris Opéra in 1836. To combat this 'lascivious tendency in stage dancing', as well as to give his fellow Copenhageners a true idea of what he considered to be genuine artistic Spanish dancing, Bournonville choreographed this extended version of *La Ventana*, combining Spanish national dances (*Seguidilla*) with pure, academic Spanish-style technique (*Pas de trois*), all held together within the frame of a charming genre picture.

La Ventana's 'non-lascivious' character was furthermore underlined by the sweet and gentle waltz-rhythms of Hans Christian Lumbye, who provided Bournonville with a score that runs in 3/4 rhythms all through the first scene, while Vilhelm Christian Holm arranged a more Spanish-influenced score for the ballet's second outdoor scene.

The photographs, which cover a period of nearly fifty years of performance, testify to the significant modifications which the Spanish dance costume underwent in that period (e.g. nos. 284, 285, 289, 290). Moreover, they reflect how the photographer occasionally attempts to create an actual stage atmosphere in the studio by adding a mirror or an appropriate back-cloth (e.g. nos. 282–284 and 288).

281 (1907). First section: '. . . The stage represents a beautiful room. In the background, a large mirror with a green curtain. To the right (first wing), a window with a Venetian blind; to the left (first wing), a white table with a flower vase and a chair . . .' (Stage director's record, 1856)

282 (c. 1871). Anna Scholl as The Señorita (4.3.1871); First section:
'... The Señorita comes dancing in, fanning herself and thinking about a young man she has met at Mass or on the Alameda. She gazes at herself in the mirror, dancing before her image ...' (*MTL*, p.176)

283 (c. 1877–79). Frederikke Madsen as The Señorita's image (4.3.1871); First section, *The mirror dance.*

284 (c. 1871) Anna Scholl as The Señorita (4.3.1871); First section:
'... However, she soon tires of this, draws the curtain across the looking glass, and pensively sits down at the table ...' (*MTL*, p.176)

285 (1907). Ellen Price de Plane as The Señorita (17.11.1902); First section:
'... Suddenly she hears sounds outside. "It is he!" [the young Señor, whom she met at the Alameda] ...' (*MTL*, p.176)

286 (1907). (cont.) '. . . She seizes her castanets and dances to the accompaniment of his melodies . . .' (*MTL*, p.176)

287 (1868). Anna Scholl as The Señorita (4.3.1871); First section: '. . . Finally she ventures over to the jalousie, pulls it aside, tosses down a topknot [as a curtsey for the rose thrown to her by the serenading Señor], and sheepishly steals away . . .' (*MTL*, p.176)

288 (1907). Second section: '. . . Changement. A garden with statues and shrubbery. In the background, steps with a balustrade across the stage. To the left (first wing), four garden chairs; to the right (fourth wing), the same . . .' (Stage director's record, 1856)

289 (1882). Charlotte Hansen (17.11.1882); Second section, *Pas de trois*: '. . . The lover, enraptured by the token he has received, calls his friends together in order to celebrate his good fortune . . .' (*MTL*, p.176)

290 (1908). Grethe Ditlevsen (4.10.1907); Second section, *Pas de trois*.

291 (1907). Ellen Price de Plane as The Señorita (17.11.1902); Second section: '. . . The Señorita enters, enveloped in her mantilla. Timid and respectful her lover approaches, repeating the refrain of his lover's lament on the guitar . . . her participation in the celebration [*Seguidilla*] is the best answer to his marriage proposal . . .' (*MTL*, p.176 ff.)

292 (c. 1862). Waldemar Price (9.10.1862); Second section, *Seguidilla*.

93

In the Carpathians

Ballet in 3 Acts.
Music by Holger Simon Paulli.
Scenery by Christian Ferdinand Christensen.
Costumes by Edvard Lehmann.
Premiered on March 4, 1857.
Last performance: March 1, 1859.
Number of performances: 15.

Among Bournonville's many 'travelogues' on foreign street life, the Hungarian ballet *In the Carpathians* stands out as his most peculiar, both with regard to its curious settings, and to the great complexity of the action.

The ballet was originally planned to be presented in Vienna during Bournonville's engagement as ballet-master at the Kärntnerthore Theatre, 1855–56. However, owing to his shortened engagement there, the idea of presenting a three-act ballet on Austrian-Hungarian folklore in the capital of that empire had to be abandoned. The project, though, was still very much alive in Bournonville's mind and, thanks to his reading of classic Hungarian literature, together with the experience of witnessing a Hungarian peasant wedding on his homeward journey, he was soon filled with renewed inspiration.

Although the ballet takes place in such different and exotic locations as the depths of a gold mine in Schemnitz (Act I), at a gipsy camp in the woodland area of the Carpathians (Act II), and at the wine harvest in Tokay (Act III), the otherwise highly dramatic action never really functioned on stage. The project therefore resulted in a ballet of a much more picturesque than dramatic nature, which may have caused most of its misfortunes. In spite of the many lively dance scenes – of which the large divertissement of Act I, named *The Pitman's Dream*, was even nominated by the critics as being Bournonville's hitherto most ingenious dance-scene – the ballet went out of the repertory after only fifteen performances. However, a number of the most popular dances survived for many years, thanks to the divertissement *The Pitman's Dream*, which Bournonville later staged as an independent ballet on November 6, 1859. Moreover, the popular *Slovanka* of Act III was incorporated as a divertissement in the first act of *The Kermesse in Brüges* on November 11, 1865, while the ballet's final *Czardas* and *Frischka* were incorporated in a later *Hungarian Divertissement*, arranged and staged by Bournonville on October 31, 1870. Thus the dances of this otherwise shortlived ballet survived on stage for nearly twenty more years after the ballet's extinction, with the *Slovanka* still being performed in today's performances of *Kermesse in Brüges*.

Owing to the ballet's short life on stage, only a very limited number of photographs are available, of which the two best are presented here. They feature two of the ballet's leading characters, the pitman Gregor (no. 293), who rebels against the drudgery of work in the gold mines, and Erzsi (no. 294), a gipsy queen and fortune-teller, who predicts the name of Gregor's beloved and reads his horoscope through a fantastic dance that prophesies his good fortune.

293 (1864). Harald Scharff as Gregor (4.3.1857); Act II, *Slovanka*.

294 (c. 1861). Petrine Fredstrup as Erzsi (4.3.1857); Act II, *Slovanka*: '... A mixed quadrille of Hungarians and gypsies, headed by Gregor and Erzsi, performs a lively Slovanka ...'

The Flower Festival in Genzano

Ballet in 1 Act.
Music by Edvard Helsted (Section I) and Holger Simon Paulli (Section II).
Scenery by Christian Ferdinand Christensen (Sets 1 and 3) and Troels Lund (Set 2.).
Costumes by August Bournonville, partly adapted from older repertory (*Napoli*, *The Festival in Albano*).
Premiered on December 19, 1858.
Last performance: November 4, 1929 (a freely adapted version with choreography by Hans Brenaa was staged at the Pantomime Theatre in the Tivoli Gardens, Copenhagen, on June 24, 1979).
Number of performances by 1929: 52 (Section II alone: 108).

The Flower Festival in Genzano, Bournonville's third Italian 'travelogue', draws on inspiration from his visits to that village in 1841 and again in 1856.

The plot is clearly divided into two main sections, with a fairly action-packed first part, followed by a dance divertissement-like second part. During his enforced exile in 1841, Bournonville, on his way to Naples, visited and conversed with the notorious pirate Gasparone, who was imprisoned in the fortress of the town of Civitavecchia and held on exhibition as a deterrent to the public and passing tourists. The experience of meeting this strange human exhibit, together with the reading of Alexandre Dumas' robber tales in *Impressions de voyage* (1833–41), was the basis for a plot that was already sketched in 1841 and resulted in a charming divertissement, which Bournonville many years later characterised in his memoirs thus: 'precisely because the ballet appeared without claiming to be a work of art, [it] was *almost* allowed to be one.'

However, the lasting popularity of this small divertissement was mostly thanks to the rich and lively succession of dances in the ballet's second section. Already by 1875 Bournonville had arranged a shortened version, to be performed separately as *Section II*. This version was actually a combination of the opening scene of the ballet (score no. 3) set together with an abridged version of the second part (score numbers 11–13 plus Finale). This arrangement became the most performed version of the ballet from 1875 to 1929, the year when the entire ballet was restaged by Kaj Smith, only to survive for one season.

Today only the famous *Pas de deux* from the ballet's second part has survived. It was originally performed by Rosa and Paolo together with a corps de ballet of eight girls, who performed decorative groups around the couple as well as dancing in between their solos. In its present, though abridged, version, the *Pas de deux* represents a true Bournonville classic by its delicate balance of natural lightheartedness and choreographic challenge. The *Pas de deux* – now long established as part of the international standard repertory – was first presented outside Denmark by Danish dancers Emilie Smith and Karl Merrild at the London Coliseum on June 8, 1914, after which the *Morning Post* reported on June 10, 1914: '[Emilie Smith] dances with surprising lightness and address, nothing being more fascinating than the delicate play of her very thin but eloquent arms. She was admirably supported by Mr Merrild, whose methods are somewhat energetic. The pas de deux, which was most favourably received, would have seemed richer and less thin had it stood for some story.'

The photographs available for *The Flower Festival in Genzano* depict mostly the ballet's second section and here in particular the *Pas de deux* and the final *Saltarello*, which is Bournonville's Roman pendant to the tarantella of *Napoli*.

The décor consisted originally of three sets (a wooded area near Arricia, the interior of an *osteria*, and the main street in Genzano), but was reduced to two sets by Bournonville on May 1, 1877. The scenery for Section I (no. 299) dates from Gustav Uhlendorff's staging of the entire ballet on October 26, 1919, while the set for Section II (no. 302) dates back to February 25, 1894, when the ballet was restaged after not having been performed for eighteen years. For this production Valdemar Gyllich arranged a new set, partly adapted from older décors (see notes for nos. 299, 302).

295 (1906). Laura Møller as Violetta (13.12.1905) and Emilie Smith as Lila (13.12.1905); Scene 1:
'. . . Young girls are binding wreaths and garlands for the festival . . .'

296 (1906). (cont.) '. . . An old woman gathers arcs and garlands into a heap . . .'

297 (c.1867). Juliette Price as Rosa (19.12.1858); Scene 1:
'. . . Gelsomina and Rosa bring baskets with bouquets, which they distribute to their friends . . .'

298 (1903). Dagny Lange as Gelsomina (23.10.1902); Scene 1.

299 (1919). Kaj Smith (26.10.1919), Edith Enna-Mathiesen (26.10.1919), Holger Mehnen (26.10. 1919), Magda Tvergaard (26.10.1919), Elna Jørgen-Jensen as Rosa (28.12.1919), Karl Merrild as Paolo (28.12.1919), Kristian Dahl (26.10.1919), Margrethe Brock-Nielsen (26.10.1919), Svend Carlo Jensen (28.12.1919), Ketty Hulstrøm (28.12.1919); Scene 2, *Ballabile*:
'. . . The stage represents a wooded area near Arricia. To the left, Rosa's house, with a picture of the Madonna. In the background, a spring rising from a grotto, above which is the road leading to Genzano . . .'

300 (c.1872–77). Marie Westberg as Rosa (11.9.1872); Scene 6:
'. . . significant glances pass between Paolo and Rosa . . .'

301 (1929). Karl Merrild as Gasparo (15.10.1929); Scene 8:
'. . . Gasparo, pondering his evil designs [to abduct Rosa], sits down at the table in a pensive mood . . .'

302 (1910). Second section, scene 12:
'. . . Transformation. We see the main street in Genzano, magnificently decorated for the Flower Festival . . .'

303 (1910). Valborg Borchsenius as Rosa (25.2.1894) and Hans Beck as Paolo (25.2.1894); Scene 12, *Pas de deux*.

304 (1902). Adeline Genée as Rosa (23.10.1902) and Hans Beck as Paolo (25.2.1894); Scene 12, *Pas de deux*.

305 (1906). Ellen Price de Plane as Rosa (27.11.1902) and Richard Jensen as Paolo (2.1.1906); Scene 12, *Pas de deux*.

306 (1906). (cont.)

307 (1929). Ulla Monti as Rosa (15.10.1929) and Harald Lander as Paolo (15.10.1929); Scene 12, *Pas de deux*.

308 (1904). Richard Jensen (23.10.1902) and Agnes Nyrop (23.10.1902); Scene 12, *Saltarello*.

309 (1919). Kaj Smith (4.6.1919), Ketty Hulstrøm (4.6.1919), Magda Tvergaard (4.6.1919), Karl Merrild (13.12.1905), Margrethe Brock-Nielsen (4.6.1919), Inger Andersen (4.6.1919), Kristian Dahl (4.6.1919), Asta Krum Hansen (4.6.1919), Holger Mehnan (4.6.1919); (lying in front) Svend Carlo Jenson (4.6.1919); Scene 12, *Saltarello*:
'. . . The procession to the church and a jubilant return. Happiness, gaiety, and dancing, which ends with: A *Saltarello* . . .'

The Mountain Hut, or Twenty Years

Romantic Ballet in 3 Tableaux (since 1866 in 2 Acts).
Music by August Winding (1st Tableau) and Emil Hartmann (2nd Tableau).
Costumes by Edvard Lehmann.
Premiered on May 13, 1859.
Last performance: May 13, 1878.
Number of performances: 28.

The Mountain Hut is Bournonville's second ballet on a Norwegian theme. It is based on the Norwegian peasant tales (*Norske Bondefortællinger*) by Norwegian writer Björnstierne Björnson, published in 1856, and more particularly on his contemporary 1857 novel *Synnöve Solbakken*. The ballet represents Bournonville's definitive break with the idiom of the Romantic Ballet, as exemplified for instance by his 1854 ballet *A Folk Tale* (see illustrations nos. 250–280), which focuses on the human mind divided under the influence of supernatural powers and an earthly existence. Against this, *The Mountain Hut* differs radically not only from *A Folk Tale*, but also from *The Wedding Festival in Hardanger* (see nos. 213–249), by having a plot of much deeper psychological realism.

The first Tableau (Act I) centres on a young peasant, Svend, who, having lost his patrimony playing cards, is lured by the corporal Christoffer to sign the enrolment list and enter the army the very same day in order to pay back his debts (see no. 310). In his desperation Svend kills the corporal (no. 312) and is forced to take flight with his fiancée, the servant maid Elna (no. 311), having been cursed by his father.

The second and third Tableaux (Act II), which take place twenty years later, centre on Svend's daughter Asta, the young sæter girl (a girl raised in the remote mountain region) who lives with her old father, now a widower, in the mountains. Asta is taken for a *Huldre* (a wood-nymph in Norwegian popular legends) by the young villagers, who cautiously avoid her and her strange old father. However, a young villager, Thorkild, is filled with deep excitement after a sudden meeting with the mysterious sæter girl, a thrill which is further strengthened when she saves him from a wounded bear which attacks him during a hunt in the mountains. Deeply moved by her courage, he leads her to the village, where she is presented as his rescuer. In the village she is introduced to the old widow Sigrid, Svend's mother, who recognises her grand-daughter by an old silver brooch, given to Asta in her childhood by her mother Elna twenty years ago. At a feast celebrating Asta's return, she dances a solo to the accompaniment of her father, who has followed his daughter to his childhood home disguised as a fiddler. Svend is soon recognised by Sigrid and received as 'the prodigal son who has returned to his mother's heart'. All curses are annulled, and the ballet ends with a jubilant wedding festival for Asta and Thorkild.

Among the ballet's many dances, Asta's solo in the third Tableau (Scene 8) stands out particularly. In a strongly emotional dance, she here expresses her inner conflict, having been raised as a child of nature in the wild mountains, but always keeping a deep instinctive feeling for her paternal roots. This solo can thus be seen in psychological terms as a *reversed* version of the solo of the troll maid Frøken Birthe in *A Folk Tale* (see nos. 273, 275, 277), who, in a similar dance in Act III of that ballet, strives against exactly the opposite instincts.

Though rather few in number, the photographs available for *The Mountain Hut* nearly all tend to create a genuine stage atmosphere, by which means the photographers wanted to emphasise the new dramatic realism of this ballet. Nos. 310, 312, and 313 are examples of this, with the last being one of the very few shots by Harald Paetz, in which he attempts to recreate an illusion of true stage performance. Here the sæter girl Asta is seen wearing her coat of bearskin, a scarlet skirt and, on her white blouse, the old silver brooch, by which she is recognised as the grand-daughter of Sigrid.

310 (c. 1865). Ludvig Gade as Svend (13.5.1859), Waldemar Price as Christoffer (9.10.1865); Axel Fredstrup as Henning (13.5.1859); First Tableau, scene 6: '. . . Henning, who discovers the playing card Svend had carelessly tossed on the table, proposes a game. Christoffer accepts his invitation. Svend is seized with the desire to wager on Henning's game, but luck is against him . . . Christoffer offers Svend his place against the unlucky Henning and stations himself behind his chair. Svend plays impetuously and loses everything . . . Christoffer praises Svend's handsome physique, and promises him glory and advancement if he will become a soldier. Svend . . . signs the recruiting papers, and immediately sits down again at the table . . .'

311 (c. 1861). Petrine Fredstrup as Elna (13.5.1859); First Tableau, scene 10:
'. . . Christoffer and Henning enter from offstage, bringing with them Svend's equipment. He is to be off this very night. This news comes as a shock to Elna [Svend's sweetheart], who has not the faintest suspicion of his enlistment . . .'

312 (c. 1865). Ludvig Gade as Svend (13.5.1859); First Tableau, scene 10:
'. . . Svend returns just as Christoffer is trying to force a kiss [from Elna]. In vain Henning tries to restrain the infuriated Svend . . . but Svend's sabre flashes. He lunges at Christoffer. A brief clash of arms is heard . . . Pale and distraught, Svend rushes across the farmyard . . . he has his revenge [in killing Christoffer] . . .'

313 (c. 1877). Athalia Flammé as Asta (27.3.1877); Second Tableau, scene 2:
'. . . [Standing alone on the spruce log with an axe in the hand and an animal skin over her head and shoulder, Asta] waves until her father [Svend] is out of sight and then tries to amuse herself in her solitude . . .'

314 (c. 1877). (cont.) Second Tableau, scene 4:
'. . . Asta has come out of the hut, seized her axe, and struck the bear such a deep blow in the back of its head that it is forced to let go of Thorkild and falls to the ground swimming in its blood . . .'

Far From Denmark, or A Costume Ball on Board

Vaudeville-Ballet in 2 Acts.
Music, in part, by Joseph Glæser.
Scenery by Troels Lund (Act I) and Christian Ferdinand Christensen (Act II).
Costumes by Edvard Lehmann.
Premiered on April 20, 1860.
Still in repertory.
Number of performances by June 1986: 438.

Bournonville's inspiration for *Far from Denmark* is drawn from two very different literary sources. Act I is his free adaptation of Friedrich Schiller's 1798 ballade *Der Handschuh*, which depicts a young northerner who is captivated by the demonic coquetry of a southern beauty and, although engaged at home, is tempted by her sensual flirtation to give up his honour. Against this, the second act takes place on the quarterdeck of a Danish frigate anchored off the South American coast, and it is an authentic recreation of a real costume ball that took place on December 30, 1840, on the Danish frigate *Bellona*, and was given as a sign of gratitude to the noble families of Buenos Aires for their warm hospitality toward the visiting Danish seamen. This historic costume ball was described in 1853 by Danish naval admiral Steen Andersen Bille, who that year published an account of his circumnavigation of the globe as commander of the Danish corvette *Galathea*.

From these varied sources Bournonville found the inspiration and atmosphere needed for a small plot that depicts a charming love intrigue between a young Danish naval officer, Wilhelm, and the roguish Rosita, daughter of the Spanish consul in Buenos Aires. At the premiere, however, the critics strongly disagreed about the ballet. Some found it an insult and a profanation of Schiller's novel, while others greatly praised Bournonville's obvious talent in evoking lively and convincing dance scenes from an otherwise trivial plot.

The audience, meanwhile, received the ballet with great enthusiasm, and this grew to almost ecstatic heights in the following years, when the Danes, having lost the 1864 war with Germany, approved this gentle vaudeville-ballet with its strong national tones, as an artistic expression of national identity, that could strengthen the country's shaken self-confidence during this difficult period. The wealth of charming national dances in Act II, which represented the different peoples and nations encountered on the frigate's circumnavigation of the globe, only added to the ballet's lasting popularity, although a number of major cuts and tightenings of plot were later considered necessary in order to keep the audience's attention during this otherwise rather lengthy genre picture. At the premiere the ballet played for nearly ninety minutes (today reduced to sixty-seven), causing one critic's rather malicious lamentation in describing *Far from Denmark* as 'a ballet which is no better than a marble sculpture with a circumference of two miles, or an abandoned drinking song with two thousand verses!!' (*Fædrelandet*, April 23, 1860).

The vast number of photographs for this ballet cover the entire performance period from its creation in 1860 right up to 1929. A special series of photographs, taken by Peter Elfelt in 1908, covers most of the mime scenes in Act I, of which only a small selection showing the most descriptive mime sequences is presented here (nos. 318–320 and 322–326). They feature the rôles of the two Danish naval cadets, Poul and Edvard, who by tradition have always been performed by ladies. Bournonville, who deeply detested the otherwise widespread use of female dancers performing *en travesti*, here plays brilliantly with this 'detestable' theatre practice, by first having the two ladies performing as Danish naval cadets and then, at the costume ball, presenting them disguised as Chinese women, and (in the Finale) as Danish girls of the island of Amager, thus creating a gently ironic pair of 'redoubled' travesty rôles.

315 (1908). Act I: '... The stage represents the veranda of a splendid villa commanding a view of the roadstead, where a Danish frigate is lying at anchor ...'

316 (1864). Juliette Price as Rosita (20.4.1860); Act I, scene 1:
'. . . As the curtain rises Rosita is seen resting in a hammock, surrounded by Negroes.
A young lady is seated at the piano, to the sounds of which two other young women,
friends of Rosita, dance, while alternately running from Rosita to a naval officer
[Wilhelm] who is sketching the aforementioned group . . .'

317 (c. 1868–72). Harald Scharff as Wilhelm, a Danish naval lieutenant (20.4.1860);
Act I.

318 (1908). Elna Lauesgaard as Edward (30.8.1908); Act I, scene 3:
'. . . Edward enters, gives a dignified salute, and delivers an invitation to a ball to
be held on board the Danish man-of-war . . .'

319 (1908). Gustav Uhlendorff as Don Alvar (1.1.1908); Act I, scene 3:
'. . . Don Alvar . . . expresses some misgivings [about Rosita's acceptance of the invitation to the ball at the Danish frigate] . . .'

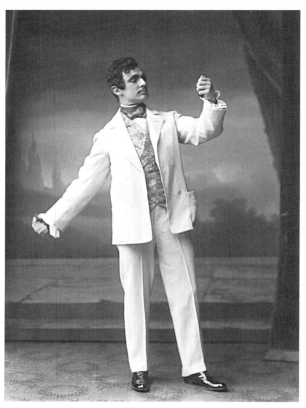

320 (1908). (cont.) Act I, scene 5: '... Medea [Rosita's maid] delivers a little box [to Don Alvar] from her mistress: it contains a pair of castanets. Overjoyed, Alvar presses them to his lips, promises to use them in the lovely lady's service, and begins to dance [a bolero] ...'

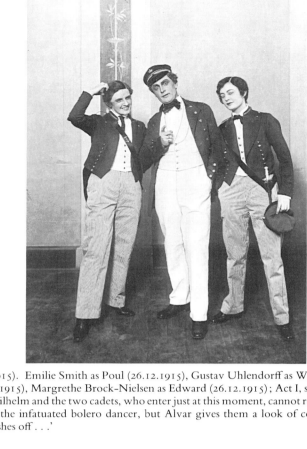

321 (1915). Emilie Smith as Poul (26.12.1915), Gustav Uhlendorff as Wilhelm (26.12.1915), Margrethe Brock-Nielsen as Edward (26.12.1915); Act I, scene 5: '... Wilhelm and the two cadets, who enter just at this moment, cannot resist making fun of the infatuated bolero dancer, but Alvar gives them a look of cold *grandeza* and rushes off ...'

322 (1908). Grethe Ditlevsen as Poul (30.8.1908); Act I, scene 6: '... Ole the Bargeman brings the mailbag, which is inspected with excitement. There is a letter for Poul ...'

323 (1868). Betty Schnell as Poul (23.10.1868) and Anna Scholl as Edward (23.10.1868); Act I, scene 6: '... but none for Edward. The latter sadly sits down at the piano and involuntarily plays the melody of the familiar song: *Across the wide ocean* ...'

324 (1908). Grethe Ditlevsen as Poul (30.8.1908) and Elna Lauesgaard as Edward (30.8.1908); Act I, scene 6:
'. . . With joy and emotion, Poul reads a letter . . .'

325 (1908). (cont.) '. . . from his beloved mother . . .'

326 (1908). (cont.) '. . . [while] Edward buries his face in his hands [not having received any news from home] . . .'

327 (1868). Betty Schnell as Poul (23.10.1868) and Anna Scholl as Edward (23.10.1868); Act I, scene 6:
'. . . The young friends, feeling that their common "mother" [Denmark] is near, enthusiastically throw themselves into each other's arms . . .'

328 (c. 1908–11). Ellen Tegner as Rosita (6.5.1899); Act I, scene 8: '. . . Rosita, in ball dress, enters . . . The party gathers [around her] for its departure [to the ball at the Danish frigate] . . .'

329 (1915). Elna Jørgen-Jensen as Rosita (26.12.1915) and Gustav Uhlendorff as Wilhelm (26.12.1915); Act I, scene 8: '. . . Wilhelm takes out his handkerchief in order to signal the bargeman [to bring them to the ball]. But in doing so, the ring [of his fiancée] falls out of his pocket and rolls onto the floor . . . Rosita tries in vain to find out who owns it. Wilhelm does not have the courage to claim it . . . She ties the ring to her fan . . .'

330 (1925). Act II: '. . . The stage represents the quarterdeck of a frigate. To right and left, gun ports, shrouds and hammock netting. At centre stage, the descent to the gun deck. Further back, the mizen-mast, the steering wheel, and the roundhouse. In the background, a gaily decorated awning . . .'

331 (c. 1868–72). Harald Scharff as Wilhelm (20.4.1860); Act II, scene 2.

332 (1864). Juliette Price as Rosita (20.4.1860); Act II, scene 2: '. . . Rosita [in ball dress] is the last to come aboard, and everyone crowds around the beautiful Argentine maid . . .'

333 (c. 1899). Alice Breitenau as an Eskimo Bride (24.4.1897); Act II, scene 4: '. . . After a quadrille danced by the naval officers together with the visiting gentlemen and their ladies, there follows a series of character dances in the following guises:1. an *Eskimo Bride* and *Bridegroom*, portrayed by two ship's boys . . .'

334 (1920). Ketty Hulstrøm as an Eskimo Bride (1.6.1920) and Svend Aage Larsen as an Eskimo Bridegroom (1.6.1920); Act II, scene 4, *Eskimo Dance*.

335 (1908). Grethe Ditlevsen as Poul, disguised as a Chinese lady (30.8.1908); Act II, scene 4:
'... *2*. a pas de cinq in Chinese style, by three Spanish gentlemen, with Poul and Edward as the ladies ...'

336 (1908). Aage Eibye (1.1.1908); Act II, scene 4, *Pas de cinq* in Chinese style.

337 (1908). Grethe Ditlevsen as Poul (30.8.1908) and Elna Lauesgaard as Edward (30.8.1908) disguised as Chinese ladies; Act II, scene 4, *Pas de cinq* in Chinese style.

338 (1920). Inger Andersen as Poul (1.6.1920), Holger Mehnen (26.12.1915), Kaj Smith (1.6.1920), Bente Hørup-Hassing as Edward (1.6.1920), Karl Merrild – in plié – (1.1.1908); Act II, scene 4, *Pas de cinq* in Chinese style.

339 (1908). Karin Lindahl as a Bayadère (1.1.1908); Act II, scene 4:
'... *3. a bayadère dance*, by [six of] Rosita's friends...'

340 (1908). Laura Møller and Tony Andersen (1.1.1908); Act II, scene 4, *Bayadère Dance*.

341 (1868). Juliette Price as Rosita (20.4.1860); Act II, scene 5:
'... Rosita, in Andalusian costume, comes out of the cabin, thanks the Captain on behalf of her countrywomen, and begins to dance: *4. a Fandango*, in which Don Alvar, the ladies, and their cavaliers take part...'

342 (1908). Ellen Tegner as Rosita (6.5.1899) and Gustav Uhlendorff as Don Alvar (1.1.1908); Act II, scene 5:
'... [Rosita] takes a rose from her hair and designates it as the prize for the best dancer. The gentlemen are vying for it... The dancing now takes on an ever more dramatic character...'

343 (1908). Gustav Uhlendorff as Don Alvar (1.1.1908); Act II, scene 4: '... Rosita looks at the hotly contested rose [snatched by the furious Alvar] with embarrassment, but Wilhelm designates Alvar as the winner of the dancing prize ...'

344 (1908). Karl Merrild as Ole the Bargeman disguised as an Indian Chieftain (1.1.1908); Act II, scene 7: '... Wild, shrill music is heard, and a new procession appears. It is Ole and five of his comrades. They perform: 5. an *Indian War Dance* ...'

345 (1920). Kristian Dahl (26.12.1915), Ketty Hulstrøm (1.6.1920), Svend Carlo Jensen (24.5.1919), Svend Aage Larsen – kneeling – (1.6.1920); Act II, scene 7, *Indian War Dance*.

346 (1908). Ellen Tegner as Rosita (6.5.1899) and Gustav Uhlendorff as Don Alvar (1.1.1908); Act II, scene 7: '... The menacing, passionate gestures [of the Indian War Dance] work on Rosita's already overwrought feelings, and she suggests to her father that it is time for them to go ... With mutual courtsey they leave the frigate at eventide as coloured lanterns are hung about the gaily decorated ship ...'

The Valkyrie

Ballet in 4 Acts.
Music by Iohan Peter Emilius Hartmann.
Scenery by Christian Ferdinand Christensen.
Costumes by Edvard Lehmann.
Premiered on September 13, 1861.
Last performance: September 29, 1921 (an abridged version by Harald
Lander, to a new score arranged by Emil Reesen and décor by Paul Kan-
neworff, was premiered on September 29, 1939, and played for seven per-
formances, with the last on October 31, 1939).
Number of performances by 1921: 122.

To understand fully the motive power that tempted Bournonville to stage
a four-act ballet based on the heroic life of ancient Scandinavia, it is important to recall his own description of this, his first venture into that genre,
as published in his 1865 memoirs only four years after the ballet's creation:
'It cannot be denied that this genre presents serious difficulties because our
present concepts of poesy have little in common with the magnificent often
grotesque forms of the Scandinavian mythology . . . To be personified [these
forms] must therefore perforce undergo modifications which inevitably lead
back to the Greek ideal.'

Although his earlier experiments had prepared him for the audience's
strong antipathy to allegoric themes, Bournonville (who rarely felt a vision
too big to treat) went with great enthusiasm into the realisation of this project from the moment the idea first struck him in the summer of 1860.

The ballet depicts the life and glorious deeds of the young Norseman
Helge, who is followed on an impending Viking expedition to the South
by his *fylgje* (guardian spirit), the valkyrie Svava, and at the end is led by
her to Valhalla, having won immortality by his death in the famous battle
on Braavalla Heath. It seems quite conceivable that Bournonville, in taking
on such a heroic theme, deliberately wanted to create a Scandinavian
counterpart to Richard Wagner's *Die Walküre*, the score of which had been

completed only five years earlier. Wagner's opera thus bears a certain motif-
affinity to Bournonville's ballet, with the relationship between Brünhilde
and Wotan paralleled by that of Svava and Odin. Moreover, Brünhilde
in the final apotheosis rides with the hero to Valhalla just as in Bournonville's
Act IV, where Helge, having won immortality in the battle at Braavalla
Heath, is led as an *Einherjar* to Valhalla by his *fylgje* Svava.

The contrasts between the ballet's many settings, reaching from the fantastic world of Norse mythology to the classic Greek temples on Sicily,
provided Bournonville with the opportunity for a diversity of dances
hitherto unknown in a single ballet. Thus the martial dances of the Valkyrie
in Act I differ strongly in both spirit and style from the Nordic dances of
the Vikings in Act II, the classic 'italianate' divertissements of the Greek
women and chieftains in Act III, and the final *Einherjar* dance in Valhalla
in Act IV.

Such contrasting choreographic characterisation of each act would, of
course, render difficult the dramatic flow, and most of the critics therefore
agreed about the weakness of the ballet's dramatic development. On the
other hand, each act observed separately was highly praised for its well-
balanced choreography and complete picturesque form. At Hans Beck's
1894 restaging of the ballet, a critic thus summed up his judgement: '*The
Valkyrie* has in choreographic richness what *Waldemar* [see nos. 15–60] has
in mimic and dramatic strength.'

Among the vast number of photographs available for *The Valkyrie* the
series showing the complete sets is of particular interest (nos. 347, 354, 361,
366, 381, 384, 387, 388) because we can follow here the scenic progress
of a long lost Bournonville ballet in all details. To keep within the epic
form Bournonville shows in these sceneries a strong preference for using
changements à vue as well as alternating between 'short' and 'deep' sets. This
preference may have been partly due to the many sudden scenic transitions
made necessary by the plot's great diversity of scenes, but as well in order
not to further hinder the already rather slow progress of the action.

347 (1905). Act I, scene 1: Opening scene with Heimdal (God of Light, personification of the Rainbow,
and sentinel of the gods) standing [see no. 348] on the rainbow – the connecting link between the gods
and the mortals.

348 (1905). Gustav Uhlendorff as Heimdal (30.12.1894); Act I, scene 1:
'. . . Heimdal sounds his Gjallar-Horn [the "shrieking horn" with which the gods are called together for their final struggle against the giants] . . .'

349 (c. 1861). Juliette Price as Svava (13.9.1861); Act I, scene 1:
'. . . [Svava and the twelve] Valkyrie perform martial dances . . .'

350 (1895). Valborg Jørgensen as Svava (1.1.1895); Act I, scene 1, *Martial Dance*.

351 (c. 1871). Waldemar Price as Odin (13.9.1861); Act I, scene 1:
'. . . The clouds part and one beholds Odin at Hlidskjálf ["Gate shelf" – Odin's watch tower in heaven from where he could survey the nine worlds] . . .'

352 (c. 1873–79). Marie Westberg as Svava (29.1.1873); Act I, scene 1: '. . . From distant lands Valhalla's bellicose maids bring tidings of battles and heroic deeds. Svava alone stands pensive and crestfallen . . .'

353 (c. 1871). Waldemar Price as Brune (13.9.1861); Act I, scene 1: '. . . Odin [henceforth among mortals under the name of Brune] has perceived this . . . He removes his sky-blue cloak and entrusts his golden armring to the goddesses. At his command the Gjallar-Horn is sounded once more, and the Valkyrie hasten away. Only Svava is detailed . . .'

354 (1905). Act I, scenes 2–7: '. . . the clouds part, [Svava] and Odin are standing in a forest on the coast of Sjælland . . .'

355 (c. 1870). Harald Scharff as Helge (13.9.1861); Act I, scene 4: '. . . The young warriors [Helge and Bjørn] enter fully equipped for the impending Viking expedition [to Sicily] . . .'

356 (c.1870). Ludvig Gade as Bjørn (13.9.1861); Act I, scene 4.

357 (1894). Hans Beck as Helge (30.12.1894); Act I, scene 4: '. . . They rejoice at the splendid long ship that is to carry them to the distant shores . . .'

358 (c. 1861). Ludvig Gade as Bjørn (13.9.1861); Act I, scene 4.

359 (c. 1870). Gerhard Döcker as Harald Hildetand (1.9.1869); Act I, scene 5:
'. . . Deeply bowed with the weight of [126] years and sorrow over his son Rerek's death, Harald Hildetand comes to have runes carved on the menhir of the fallen warrior . . .'

360 (1906). Oscar Iversen as Bjørn (31.8.1905); Act I, scene 6:
'. . . Bjørn enters with Helge's men. He salutes [Harald Hildetand] respectfully, points toward the beach [for the imminent Viking expedition] and raises his javelin while the men strike their shields . . .'

361 (1905). Act II: '. . . A rock cave on the coast of Brittany. In the background, the sea . . .'

362 (1894). Hans Beck as Helge (30.12.1894) and Waldemar Price as Bjørn (30 12.1894); Act II, scene 1:
'. . . Helge has been wounded in the arm. Bjørn perceives this and wishes to dress the wound. But as their eyes meet they are both struck with the same idea: they will become blood-brothers . . .'

363 (1894). (cont.) '. . . The warriors form a circle about them and, with the solemnity which attends this ancient custom, Helge and Bjørn vow to live and die as loyal friends . . .'

364 (1919). Gustav Uhlendorff as Helge (26.12.1919) and Elna Jørgen-Jensen as Svava (26.12.1919); Act II, scene 2:
'. . . Svava [transformed into a swan] flies over the sea, dives down and rises from the waves in another guise . . . she tenderly beholds the wounded [sleeping] Helge, pours balsam on his arm and heals it. Helge awakens . . .'

365 (c. 1894–96). Anna Harboe as Svava (30.12.1894); Act II, scene 2:
'. . . "Be mine!" he exclaims. "Come with me to the land of my ancestors." Svava indicates that he must first win a hero's name. "Will thy love then be my reward?" Svava points toward the heavens. Helge ponders the meaning of this sign . . .'

366 (1905). Act III: '. . . A magnificent garden at Catania, on Sicily. In the background can be seen the bay; to the right a kiosk in the form of a temple . . .'

367 (1919). In centre: Gustav Uhlendorff as Helge (26.12.1919) and Richard Jensen as Nicetas (26.12.1919) surrounded by Greek chieftains and slaves; Act III, scene 1: '. . . Helge has been given a friendly reception by the Byzantine Viceregent, Nicetas, who has arranged a feast in his honour. At a splendid table the Nordic sea-king is served . . .'

368 (1919). Karl Merrild as a Greek chieftain (26.12.1919); Act II, scene 1: '. . . The Greek chieftains vie to pay him the most flattering homage . . . and loud music intoxicates the overwhelmed senses . . .'

369 (c. 1905). Elna Lauesgaard as a Greek *danseuse* (31.8.1905); Act III, scene 1: '. . . Nicetas gives a signal, the table is taken away, the slaves and honour guard withdraw. The Temple opens and out steps a chorus of [twelve] graceful maidens, who shall heighten the festivity by their dancing . . .'

370 (c. 1905). Ellen Tegner as a Greek *danseuse* (31.8.1905); Act III, scene 1: '. . .The music sounds, and the dances alternate with hilarious jesting, during which the maidens hide Helge's weapons in the kiosk and adorn him with flowers . . .'

371 (c. 1861). Juliette Price as Svava (13.9.1861); Act III, scene 2: '. . . An unknown young woman brings a basket of fruit . . .'

372 (1895). Valborg Jørgensen as Svava (1.1.1895); Act III, scene 2:
'. . . which she distributes among those who curiously gather round her . . .'

373 (c. 1870). Betty Schnell as Svava (1.9.1869); Act III, scene 2:
'. . . only an apple does she keep . . .'

374 (c. 1894–96). Anna Harboe as Svava (30.12.1894); Act III, scene 2:
'. . . and lifts it just as she pauses in front of Helge. So intoxicated with pleasure
is he, that he has failed to notice her presence. Thus his surprise is all the greater
when he recognises the gentle features which . . . on the coast of Brittany, made
such a deep impression on his heart! . . .'

375 (c. 1894–96). (cont.) '. . . The [Greek] men are captivated by her dancing, even
though it is quite different from that of the Greek women. The latter express their
jealousy over the applause accorded the foreign maid . . .'

376 (c. 1870). Ludvig Gade as Bjørn (13.9.1861); Act III, scene 4:
'. . . Greek women steal up behind Bjørn and poke fun at the boorish Norseman. They soon go further and offer him wine. Bjørn thanks them and inquires after Helge, but they answer evasively and continue to fill his cup while dancing about him . . .'

377 (1906). Oscar Iversen as Bjørn (31.8.1905); Act III, scene 4:
'. . . His countenance gradually softens. He drinks one glass after another, allows himself to be disarmed and entwined with garlands and dances off with the maidens in a bacchantic chain that winds its way through the sinuous garden paths . . .'

378 (1883). Oscar Iversen (1.9.1869), Arnold Walbom (29.1.1873), Fritz Gold (5.9.1876) as Greek chieftains and Emil Hansen as Nicetas (29.1.1873); Act III, scene 7:
'. . . Nicetas, who thought he could take the unarmed Norseman by surprise, flies into a rage when he learns that they have ensconced themselves in the temple. His warriors wish to storm it, but he knows a surer way of coercing the foreigners . . .'

379 (1864). Harald Scharff as Helge (13.9.1861); Act III, scene 7:
'. . . their place of refuge is surrounded with bundles of brushwood, trees and other combustible materials which are lighted by the women . . . But suddenly the temple doors fly open and Helge and his Vikings toss their shields over the fire, leap through the crackling flames and, with heavy blows, cut into the terrified Greeks . . .'

380 (1919). Elna Jørgen-Jensen as Svava (26.12.1919) and corps de ballet as Valkyrie; Act III, scene 7:
'. . . like a gust of wind, a host of shield-maidens darts forward against the traitors, causing them to flee in every direction. Svava stands triumphant among the proud Valkyrie . . . Helge's ship heads home for the great battle of the North . . .'

381 (1905). Act IV, scenes 1–2: '. . . Bravalla Heath at dawn. To the right, King Harald's tent; to the left, a rampart with the King's standard and some military engines. The extensive backdrop shows distant, wood-covered hills . . .'

382 (c. 1861). Juliette Price as Svava (13.9.1861); Act IV, scene 1: '. . . Svava, armed as a shieldmaiden, stands at [Brune's] side . . .'

383 (c. 1894). Ludvig Gade as Harald Hildetand (30.12.1894); Act IV, scene 1: '. . . Harald Hildetand, in full battle dress, emerges from his tent . . . He is greeted by the clanging of arms and responds with dignity to the army's jubilant acclamation . . .'

384 (1905). Act IV, scenes 3–5: 'Transformation. A spruce forest [here birch wood and, in the background, *Hlidskjálf*, Odin's watch tower in heaven]. The tumult of battle is expressed by the music throughout the ensuing action . . .'

385 (1867). Juliette Price as Svava (13.9.1861); Act IV, scene 3:
'. . . With wild delight, Svava and the Valkyrie dash through the forest . . .'

386 (c.1869). Emilie Bryde as a Valkyrie (1.9.1869); Act IV, scene 3:
'. . . They meet, brandish their spears and point toward the [Bravalla] heath, where death is raging. They hasten away in a jubilant dance . . .'

387 (1905). Act IV, scene 7: '. . . Transformation. Darkness has settled over the heath, and the roar of the storm has replaced the dying din of battle . . . Heimdal's Gjallar-Horn sounds. The mist of night vanishes . . .'

388 (1905). Act IV, the final scene: '. . . [Valhalla in Gimle – the Paradise of the pagans] the fallen heroes cast off their bloody garb. Radiance surrounds them, and they stand in Valhalla as *einherjar* [Odin's companions], clad in light, glittering armour with winged helmets . . .'

389 (1905). At the staircase: Valborg Guldbrandsen as Svava (1.1.1895) and Hans Beck as Helge (30.12.1894); (on the High-Seat) Holger Holm as Odin (31.8.1905) and Anna Agerholm as a Goddess (31.8.1905); Act IV, the final scene: '. . . Valfather [Odin: Father of the Slain] has called his chosen ones to him . . . Svava hands Helge the cup of immortality. Now she shall belong forever to the hero whose *fylgja* she was. The Valkyrie step forth . . . and the *einherjar* perform warlike games and acclaim their Heerfather [Odin: Father of the Host] with a shield dance . . .'

Pontemolle

Vaudeville-Ballet in 2 Tableaux.
Music composed and arranged by Vilhelm Christian Holm (First Tableau) and, partly, by Andreas Frederik Lincke (Second Tableau).
Scenery by Christian Ferdinand Christensen.
Costumes arranged by Edvard Lehmann.
Premiered on April 11, 1866.
Last performance: November 21, 1911.
Number of performances: 64.

Pontemolle, Bournonville's fourth and last Italian 'travelogue', was created on the occasion of the forty-eighth birthday of King Christian IX on April 8, 1866.

However, the inspiration which spurred Bournonville in 1866 to choreograph a ballet on a larger scale than the divertissement trifles usually mounted for such Royal red-letter days, was the impressive number of young and highly talented dancers he was met with in the Royal Danish Ballet on his return from three seasons in Stockholm, where he had served as managing director of the Royal Swedish Opera.

The ballet, which was given the status of Vaudeville-Ballet with the explicit purpose of not having it judged as just an occasional work, was, in fact, received with great acclaim and enthusiasm, and reached the rather remarkable number of sixty-four performances over a span of fifty-five years.

Clearly referring to Bournonville's own Roman sojourn in the summer of 1841, the action depicts a colony of Danish artists in Rome, who, after a number of innocent love intrigues with the local Roman beauties, gather at the famous inn La Storta at the ancient Ponte Milvio, north of Rome, to celebrate a *Pontemolle* (an artists' farewell party). On this occasion it is for the Danish painter Alfred, who is about to return to his native country. At the party a carnival procession is arranged, which opens with a pas de deux performed by the Roman beauty, Camilla, whom all the Danish artists have depicted in some kind of a portrait competition. However, with her pas de deux Camilla (photo no. 399) takes all her Danish worshippers by surprise by suddenly introducing her Roman sweetheart, Fabriccio, into the midst of the Danish colony. There follows a series of dances depicting the different epochs in the history of Roman art, reaching from Ancient Rome through the Renaissance to end with the Rococo period. At the ballet's end everybody salutes the departing Alfred and in the middle of a roaring gallopade a train is seen crossing the distant bridge of Ponte Milvio (see no. 397), with the artist waving to his Italian friends with the Danish flag, now well on his way toward the far North.

Although rather limited in number, the photographs available for *Pontemolle* all testify to the undiminished skill and youthful charm with which the sixty-year-old Bournonville so brilliantly choreographed what was to become his last Italian genre picture. The ballet's picturesque charm can be glimpsed in particular from the series of photographs depicting the jealousy scene between Camilla and Fabriccio (nos. 391–395), as well as from the large number of character dances (nos. 399–402), not forgetting the poetic décor of the artist Alfred's Roman atelier (no. 390), and the landscape near the bridge of Ponte Milvio outside Rome (no. 397).

390 (1905). First Tableau: '. . . An artist's atelier in Rome. The locale was once a splendid hall open onto a perron and garden. In the background can be seen a portion of the city. Doors to the right and left. The light, which comes from above, is filtered through a sunshade. Picturesque disarray. Sketches, busts, weapons, old furniture, and ethnographic objects . . .'

391 (1906). Ellen Price de Plane as Camilla (3.12.1905); First Tableau, scene 5:
'. . . Camilla beckons to the old *scrivano* [Paoluccio] and dictates a letter to him [for the departing Danish artist, Alfred, who has portrayed her so brilliantly] . . .'

392 (1907). Gustav Uhlendorff as Fabriccio (3.12.1906) and Grethe Ditlevsen as Camilla (8.3.1907); First tableau, scene 5:
'. . . Fabriccio [Camilla's sweetheart] slips in from the perron and hides behind [the painter] Cesar's cartoon in order to spy on Camilla [who is dictating her farewell letter for Alfred to the old *scrivano* Paoluccio] . . .'

393 (1907). (cont.) First Tableau, scene 6:
'. . . A scene of amazement, frolicking, jealousy . . .'

394 (1907). (cont.) '. . . and reconciliation . . .'

395 (1907). (cont.) '. . . between Fabriccio and Camilla . . .'

HERR HANS BECK OG FRU VALBORG GULDBRANDSEN.

396 (c. 1905). Valborg Guldbrandsen as Annina (3.12.1905) and Hans Beck as Chauvin (3.12.1905); First Tableau, scene 7:
'. . . Annina [Camilla's sister] enters pursued by [the regimental drummer] Chauvin, who is assuring her of his sincere love . . . and when he . . . promises her a future as a *vivandière* with the Cross of the *Légion d'Honneur* at her breast, she is won over to his marriage plan, takes his arm, and marches about with him . . .'

397 (1905). Second Tableau: '. . . A landscape outside Rome (in the vicinity of the old Pons Milvius, well known from the defeat of the Emperor Maximus, and later christened Ponte Molle). To the left, the inn called La Storta, where artists' parties of welcome and farewell are customarily held. To the right, in the foreground, the ruins of an ancient temple . . .'

398 (1867). Ludvig Gade as Chauvin (11.4.1866); Second Tableau, scene 2: '. . . A grand procession headed by Chauvin, in dress uniform, and the French military band . . .'

399 (1906). Ellen Price de Plane as Camilla (3.12.1905); Second Tableau, scene 2, *Pas de deux* and *Saltarello*: '. . . A signal is given for the dancing to begin, and in the following order are performed: A *pas de deux* and *Saltarello* [by Camilla and Fabriccio] . . .'

400 (c. 1875–79). Charlotte Schousgaard as the leading Flower Maiden (21.10.1875); Second Tableau, scene 2: '. . . *Ancient Rome* – [depicted in a dance performed by two] Gladiators and [seven] Flower Maidens . . .'

401 (c. 1870). Laura Stillmann as Annina (11.4.1866); Second Tableau, scene 2: '. . . The Age of Art (from the sixteenth century) – [depicted in the performance of a] *Rococo Quadrille* . . .'

402 (1908). Karl Merrild as Pulcinello (3.12.1905); Second Tableau, scene 2:
'. . . *Pulcinello* – an indispensable grotesque figure . . .'

403 (1905). Holger Holm as Alfred (3.12.1905); Second Tableau, scene 3:
'. . . [Alfred's] native land beckons him with its waving flag . . . Deeply moved
by this unexpected and solemn movement, Alfred hangs the wreath [offered him
by three little girls dressed as genii] on the sacred symbol of his native land . . .
and hastens off – to the North! to the North! . . .'

404 (1905). Centre group: Hans Beck as Chauvin (3.12.1905), Valborg Guldbrandsen as Annina (3.12.1905), Frederikke Madsen as Fulvia (3.12.1905),
Ellen Price de Plane as Camilla (3.12.1905), Gustav Uhlendorff as Fabriccio (3.12.1905); (above them) Karl Merrild as Pulcinello (3.12.1905) and corps
de ballet; Second Tableau, scene 4:
'. . . Joy appears to have been struck dumb by Alfred's departure . . . but Chauvin orders the drum to be beaten, and the French military band
strikes up a thunderous galopade. Life springs anew into the numerous crowd, and dancing helps to dispel the heavy clouds of sadness . . .'

The Lay of Thrym

Ballet in 4 Acts with a Final Tableau.
Music by Iohan Peter Emilius Hartmann.
Scenery by Christian Ferdinand Christensen (Act I, Act III and Final Tableau) and Fritz Ahlgrensson (Act II, Act IV).
Costumes by Edvard Lehmann.
Premiered on February 21, 1868.
Last performance: May 16, 1905 (Act I was performed separately three times in the season 1914–15 and, in a shortened version, at a charity performance at the Casino Theatre, Copenhagen, on April 4, 1919).
Number of performances by 1905: 73.

The Lay of Thrym, Bournonville's most ambitious ballet project ever, became his greatest achievement within the genre of Nordic mythology. Throughout his life he had devoured the poetic and dramatic works by the Danish poet Adam Oehlenschläger, and with the positive experience of *The Valkyrie* in 1861 he was spurred with renewed inspiration for an even greater balletic work in this sphere. This was to be woven together from various sources, such as Oehlenschläger's 1818 Eddaic cycle *Gods of the North* and the historical writings by Finn Magnussen and Nicolai Frederik Severin Grundtvig.

The ballet's most important plot complications, however, were taken from the Icelandic sagas and in particular that of *The Lay of the Giant Thrym*, which tells of the giant Thrym, who, with the help of the cunning As Loke, succeeds in tricking the magic hammer, Mjollnir, from the mighty As Thor. Delighted at having the hammer in his power, Thrym now wants to propose to the goddess Freia (no. 412). Meanwhile, Loke has deceitfully arranged to have Thor appear at the wedding disguised as Freia, with himself dressed as one of the goddess' maidservants (no. 418), thus trying to win back the hammer from the giant by luring him to offer it as a wedding present to his future 'bride'. His power now restored, Thor attacks the giant and with this struggle begins the final fall of the gods, as depicted in the chaotic destruction of Ragnarok. In the ballet's final tableau the glorification of the gods in a new and better world is depicted with the marriage ceremony of the gods Baldur and Nanna taking place in the idyllic harmony of Gimle – the Paradise of the pagans.

At the ballet's premiere the entire critical establishment found this massive work just as troublesome as impressive. As with *The Valkyrie*, it seemed to the reviewers that the vast numbers of characters needed for the great complexity of the plot worked rather against the ballet's dramatic flow, thereby resulting in a series of separate scenes of magnificent visual effect which, however, never really united into a dramatic whole. The critic of *Berlingske Tidende* (February 22, 1868) found the plot, by focusing on the Dionysian character of Loke – the ballet's absolute dominating character – too uneven in style. A true drama within this mythological sphere would, according to that critic, have been better depicted, had more emphasis been given to a confrontation between the Dionysian personality of Loke in opposition to that of the Apollonian gods, a theme also to be found within the Norse mythology. The critic thus suggested that Bournonville should have interpolated some of the myths from *The Lay of Baldur* into the actual drama of this ballet, and not simply, as was the case, have the Apollonian god Baldur appearing in the allegorical Final Tableau.

However, thanks to Hartmann's brilliant score, the impressive décors (especially the two sets by Swedish scene painter Fritz Ahlgrensson), and Bournonville's unerring talent for mounting large-scale scenarios of previously unknown stage effects, the ballet was an extraordinary box-office success and was kept in the repertory for nearly forty years. Though limited in number, the photographs available for *The Lay of Thrym* cover the entire performance period from the ballet's 1868 creation to its last production in 1901. They focus on the leading characters, the deceitful Loke, his faithful bride Sigyn, the boorish giant Thrym, and the mighty As Thor.

The Norns

Prologue to August Bournonville's Ballet *The Lay of Thrym*
Text by Hans Peter Holst.
Music by Iohan Peter Emilius Hartmann.
Premiered on February 21, 1868.
Last performance: May 22, 1874.
Number of performances: 41.

Although intended as an explanatory curtain-raiser to the ballet's complicated plot, Holst's prologue for five actors and an unseen chorus with music by Hartmann was only marginally successful.

With the depiction of a Norwegian viking, Eigil, who tells his wife, Ausa (no. 405), of his conversion to Christianity, set together with a final scene of the three Norns, who predict the fall of the Nordic gods, the critics found the prologue working more against the ballet's plot than actually clarifying it. *Fædrelandet* (February 24, 1868) stated: 'A setting for instance in an Icelandic log hut, where the old Eddaic cycles originally were written, would have been much more suitable as a prologue for the complicated plot of this ballet, while Holst's present text and settings nearly mistreats both Norse mythology and Christianity, by employing both in such shallowish manner.' As a result of this consistent criticism the prologue was finally abandoned in 1874.

405 (c. 1870). Agnes Lange as Ausa (21.2.1868); Prologue, The Norns: '. . . Ausa (who has listened [to the unseen chorus] with horror): O, dreadful news! Whence comest those tones which the death do portend of Valhalla? It shall fall into ruins and, then, like a star, it shall be extinguished forever! . . .'

406 (1919). Emilie Walbom as Vola (12.9.1902), Edith Enna-Mathiesen (4.4.1919) Carla Keller (16.5.1915) Magda Tvergaard (16.5.1915) Elna Hansen (4.4.1919) and Emilie Smith (16.5.1915) as Vola's five foster daughters, Richard Jensen as Asa-Loke (4.4.1919); Act I, scene 2:
'. . . Asa-Loke appears [in the cave of the wise-woman Vola]. All bow to his power and, at a sign from him, Vola is forced to summon her five young foster daughters. To the first Loke hands a *mirror*; To the second, *an arrow* [seen here]; To the third, *a brimming cup*; To the fourth, *fragrant flowers*; And finally, to the fifth, *a glockenspiel*. This test of the [five] senses provides the opportunity for a dance . . .'

407 (1919). Unidentified person as Thiase, a fire spirit (4.4.1919), Emilie Walbom as Vola (12.9.1902). Richard Jensen as Asa-Loke (4.4.1919), unidentified person as Finn, a fire spirit (4.4.1919); Act I, scene 3:
'. . . Vola has a sixth foster daughter, the gladsome Sigyn, whom she has endeavoured to keep from Loke's notice. But he demands to see her and, when Vola anxiously and suspiciously points to the drink which has already been poured into golden cups, he assures her that Sigyn shall be sacred to him, for he has chosen her to be his wife. Vola hesitates to fulfill his wish, but with a single sign [to the fire spirits] the Lord of Fire conjures up an extraordinary brightness . . .'

408 (1901). Hans Beck as Asa-Loke (14.5.1895) and Valborg Guldbrandsen as Sigyn (14.5.1895); Act I, scene 4:
'. . . Sigyn comes dancing in and asks her mother what has caused this radiance . . . Loke steps forth, reassures the astonished maiden and . . . tries to win her heart. Sigyn is easily deceived by the cunning god's entreaties and declarations . . .'

409 (1919). Richard Jensen as Asa-Loke (4.4.1919), Elna Jørgen-Jensen as Sigyn (4.4.1919), Emilie Walbom as Vola (12.9.1902); Act I, scene 4:
'. . . He binds her to him with a golden chain and, paying no heed to Vola's forebodings, she confidently places her hand in Loke's . . .'

410 (c. 1870). Waldemar Price as Thor (21.2.1868); Act I, scene 5:
'. . . A tremendous thunderclap is heard . . . A boat is tossing on the rough waves. Thor stands tall in the stern . . .'

411 (1904). Holger Holm as Thor (13.1.1901); Act I, scene 5:
'. . . Thor, beside himself with wrath, hurls his hammer, Mjollnir, after his escaped quarry [the Midgard Serpent] . . .'

412 (1901). Oscar Iversen as Thrym (2.9.1886) and Hans Beck as Asa-Loke (14.5.1895); Act I, scene 7:
'. . . Thrym [King of the Giants] expresses his dejection at finding himself alone. Without a wife! Without love! Loke promises to show him the ideal woman and touching the giant's eyelid, he puts him into a deep trance . . .'

413 (c. 1870). Josephine Eckardt as Freia (21.2.1868); Act I, scene 7:
'. . . In [Thrym's] mind's eye a magnificent sight unfolds: Freia's hall, where the goddess, surrounded by the Disir [fate-goddesses] and light elves, receives her brother [Freir] who brings a bride from the realm of the giants to the home of the Vanir [the Giants] . . .'

414 (c. 1870). Johanne Petersen as Gerda, in bridal dress (21.2.1868); Act I, scene 7:
'. . . The lovely Gerda kneels before Freia who raises her up into her embrace and bestows her blessing upon her and upon Freir [by presenting them with two white pigeons]. The Disir remove Gerda's subterranean headdress and adorn her with the bridal wreath . . .'

415 (1901). Hans Beck as Asa-Loke (14.5.1895); Act I, scene 9:
'. . . Thrym orders a high-seat erected; behind it Loke conceals himself in order to surreptitiously give secret counsels to the King of the Giants . . .'

416 (c. 1870). Betty Schnell as Sigyn (21.8.1868); Act III, scene 1, Freia's sacred grove:
'. . . Sigyn, in the service of the Goddess, waters her flowers . . .'

417 (c.1870). (cont.) '. . . and sadly dwells on the one [Loke] she cannot tear out of her heart in spite of all his faults . . .'

418 (1901). Hans Beck as Asa-Loke (14.5.1895); Act IV, scene 2, Thrym's subterranean royal hall:
'. . . [Loke disguised as] the eager maidservant [of the also disguised Thor, who appears as Sigyn] praises the goddess's lovely countenance . . .'

419 (c. 1870). Betty Schnell as Sigyn, with the bridal crown (21.2.1868); Act IV, scene 4:
'. . . Sigyn enquires [of Vola] for her husband [Loke] pointing at the golden chain . . .' (*Répétiteur*, KTB 299, p.114)

420 (c. 1871). (cont.) '... Vola [being against her daughter's union with Loke] removes the chain from Sigyn's neck. Sigyn: "But why? – he is the one I love!" ...' (*Répétiteur*, KTB 299, p.114)

421 (c. 1871). (cont.) '... Sigyn will pick up the chain but is hindered by Vola, who again throws it far away and threatens Sigyn to bestow her curse upon her ...' (*Répétiteur*, KTB 299, p.114)

422 (c. 1872). Marie Westberg as Sigyn (17.9.1871); Act IV, scene 4: '... The hour of [Loke's] punishment and reckoning has come! The Aesir bind him with the very chain with which Loke captivated Sigyn. In vain, Sigyn begs them for mercy [for the deceitful Loke] ...'

423 (c. 1872). (cont.) Act IV, scene 5: '... From the midst [of Ragnarok] rises a dead tree, from whose branches a poisonous snake hangs down over Loke, who is bound to the rock by fire spirits ... The faithful wife will share his suffering! ... supporting Loke's head, she holds the bowl beneath the serpent's jaws in order to catch the dripping venom ...'

The King's Corps of Volunteers on Amager
– An Episode From 1808

Vaudeville-Ballet in 1 Act.
Music composed and arranged by Vilhelm Christian Holm.
Scenery by Valdemar Gyllich.
Costumes by Edvard Lehmann.
Premiered on February 19, 1871.
Still in repertory.
Number of performances by June 1986: 370.

Bournonville's last ballet within the genre of Vaudeville-Ballet was based on the then sixty-five-year-old choreographer's early childhood memories.

On the island of Amager, south of Copenhagen, Bournonville used to spend his childhood school holidays with a colony of Dutch farmers. Here he came to know the farmers' rich national festive customs, carefully preserved since the sixteenth century, when a colony of Dutch farmers had been invited by King Christian IV to settle on Amager in order to cultivate the rich soils of that island. These early childhood memories were later described in Bournonville's memoirs *My Theatre Life*, and while writing this, Bournonville was caught by the idea of creating a ballet set in this picturesque milieu – which had also been depicted in the popular genre paintings of Danish artist Julius Exner.

The ballet's plot, however, was based on the history of the King's Corps of Volunteers – a kind of voluntary Home Guard founded in 1801, when Denmark was at war with England. Among the many prominent members of this Guard were Bournonville's father, Antoine Bournonville, and the famous French singer and concert-master at Copenhagen's Royal Theatre at that time, Edouard Du Puy (1770–1822), the latter serving as model for the ballet's main character, Edouard.

Du Puy was the first singer in Denmark to perform the rôle of Don Juan in Mozart's opera, a character he seems to have played with equal enthusiasm in the social life of Copenhagen as well as on stage. In 1809 he was exiled on the direct order of the King, after it was discovered that he had formed an intimate relationship with the King's daughter-in-law, Princess Charlotte Frederikke, whom Du Puy had taught music and – apparently – other things. Being exiled, however, Du Puy almost immediately became a legendary figure in Danish theatre history, and Bournonville, who always had a keen eye for what might work within the gentle genre of Vaudeville-Ballet, soon capitalised on this real Don Juan personality by depicting him in an amiable plot, centring on a small love intrigue provoked by Edouard's flirtations with the young Amager girls during the time the King's Corps of Volunteers is billeted on that island.

Among the twelve photographs presented here, that of the ballet's scenery (no. 424) is of particular interest. It serves as a fine example of how little the sceneries of Bournonville's ballets were actually changed in the first fifty years after his death. The reason for this rather conservative holding on to the original décors must be explained as a strange mixture of economic necessity and a true veneration for the ballet's scenic traditions (see note for no. 424). Note also the sophisticated lighting of the décor, here imitating the snow covered landscape's reflections of light into the Amager farmhouse parlour, by using strong stage lights from below (!). Finally, the uniform of Edouard as seen on photograph 426 is an exact replica of the uniform worn by the King's Corps of Volunteers, of which Bournonville himself became a member in 1848.

424 (1905). Scenes 1–12 (Finale): '. . . The stage represents the parlour of a prosperous farmhouse (in which a Lieutenant and an *Overjæger* of the King's Corps of Volunteers are billeted). To the right, a stove fed from another room [*bilæggerovn*], a piano, and a bed in an alcove. To the left, an oak table and cupboard. Doors on both sides; the right-hand one leads outdoors, while that to the left gives access to the other rooms. The background is formed by a garden door and two windows, through which can be seen a flat winter landscape and, in the distance, the seashore. Along the walls, old-fashioned furniture and benches which can be used for sleeping [*slagbænke*] . . .'

425 (c. 1890). Charlotte Hansen as Else (22.1.1887), Elisabeth Soyer as Bodil (2.3.1887) and Eleonora Monti as Trine (25.1.1890); scene 1:
'. . . Else and Trine are decorating a ridiculously outfitted doll [for the merry Shrovetide celebration]. Bodil comes in [and sees the funny doll the girls have made] . . .'

426 (1907). Hans Beck as Edouard (8.3.1905); scene 3:
'. . . The Volunteers are heard returning after having made their rounds of the coast. They halt outside the farmhouse. Everyone rushes to the windows and the garden door is opened for Lieutenant Edouard [in full armour], who, after turning over his command, enters . . .'

427 (c. 1871). Waldemar Price as Edouard (19.2.1871); scene 4:
'. . . Edouard sits down in an armchair and reads himself to sleep, but is soon disturbed by a melody that continues to haunt him. He tries in vain to find some peace, but it is no use . . .'

428 (1905). Ellen Braunstein as Else (8.3.1905) and Richard Jensen as Dirck (8.3.1905); scene 7:
'. . . Else sits down in a corner to weep while the lad anxiously paces the floor. He gives vent to his dejection by reproaching the girl for her coquetry [with the Volunteers] . . .'

429 (c. 1899). Agnes Mibach as Trine (13.2.1899) and Ellen Price as Else (13.2.1899); scene 10:
'. . . Angrily the girls [decide] to explain [to Louise] that it is not these two gentlemen [Otto and Emil] who are responsible for the farmhands' [Jan's and Dirck's] jealousy, but, rather, the Lieutenant [Edouard] who was always talking and singing of love!...'

430 (c. 1877–85). Frederikke Madsen as a *Vivandière* (6.1.1874); scene 11, *Polka Militaire*:
'. . . Four masked hussar *vivandières* ask the same number of Volunteers to dance – namely, Steffen, Otto, Carl, and Edouard . . .'

431 (1912). Karl Merrild as Otto (26.12.1910); scene 11, *Polka Militaire*.

432 (1905). Richard Jensen as Dirck (8.3.1905); scene 11:
'. . . PAS DE TROIS performed by Emil [here Dirck disguised as Prince Carnival], Else, and Trine [disguised as goddesses of Folly] . . .'

433 (1905). Emilie Smith as Andrea (8.3.1905); scene 11:
'... PAS DE TROIS performed by Emil [disguised as Prince Carnival], Else [here Andrea], and Trine [disguised as goddesses of Folly] ...'

434 (c. 1889). Hans Beck as Emil (5.3.1889); scene 11, *The Reel*:
'... a whole corps de ballet made up of [four] natives of Amager [girls] and [three] Volunteers [performs a Reel] ...'

435 (1918). Inger Andersen (4.6.1918), Harry Larsen (11.11.1916), Karla Keller (4.6.1918), Karl Merrild (11.11.1916), Holger Mehnen (4.6.1918), Elna Hansen (4.6.1918), Aage Eibye (4.6.1918), Bente Hørup-Hassing (4.6.1918); scene 11, *The Reel*.

The Mandarin's Daughters

Ballet Divertissement.
Music arranged and composed by Vilhelm Christian Holm.
Costumes by Edvard Lehmann.
Premiered on April 23, 1873.
Last performance: October 25, 1875.
Number of performances: 14.

The Mandarin's Daughters was originally conceived only as a dance divertissement set in the exotic sphere of sixteenth-century China. For repertory reasons, however, this plan was extended, so that the piece became ranked as a Ballet Divertissement with a plot and large number of dances, playing for a total of forty-five minutes.

Having created a small ballet from Hans Christian Andersen's popular fairy-tale *The Steadfast Tin Soldier* in 1871, Bournonville now wanted to stage a similar fairy-tale ballet within the exotic atmosphere of another of Andersen's popular tales, the Chinese adventure *The Nightingale*. It was, however, only Andersen's vivid description of Imperial China that spurred Bournonville to choreograph in this exotic sphere: the ballet's action was set up by himself. It depicts a Chinese Prince who is about to choose his future wife from among the three rival daughters of the Mandarin Kao-Li. However, when the shy and humble daughter of the Mandarin's consort appears, the Prince immediately changes his mind and chooses her as his bride. The marriage contract is now sealed with a game of chess, performed by living chessmen on a floor carpet of chess squares. After the Prince's victory in the chess game, the festivities end with a parade of Chinese lanterns, beneath which the Prince leads the humble young Ping-Sin home as his bride.

The choreographic highlight was *The Ballet of the Chessmen*, performed by thirty-two dancers (sixteen children and sixteen adults), who were directed by the Prince and the young bride's father from an erected platform in the background. This dance was described by a critic as 'a completely new and delightful innovation. It opens with a series of moves by which the fallen chessmen are carried out as dead and stiffened bodies. As the game progresses the officers of the winning part begin to dance more and more wildly to end up in a threatening group around the checkmate King.' (*Berlingske Tidende*, April 24, 1875). Furthermore, in the divertissement's final section Bournonville played with the continuous effect of having a large number of chessmen falling upon each other like dominoes, to symbolise one of the players having the upper hand in the game.

Bournonville was not the first, however, to invent a 'living chessmen' ballet. In 1858 a similar scene had been staged by Joseph Mazilier in his ballet *La Magicienne*, premiered at the Paris Opéra on March 17, 1858. Bournonville had seen this piece in Paris, and we can therefore assume that *The Ballet of the Chessmen* must, at least in part, have been based on Mazilier's choreography. Some of the ballet's other dances were also taken from older works, though these were Bournonville's own. The dance of the Mandarin's three daughters, as well as a number of corps de ballet dances, were taken from the second act of his 1855 Persian ballet *Abdallah*. It could look, at first sight, as if Bournonville was not troubled at all by employing older Persian-style choreography in a new Chinese setting, but the reason for this extensive recycling of older choreography must have been due, in part, to the time pressure under which he was working when having to expand this divertissement, with only very short notice, into a large forty-five-minute ballet at the request of the theatre management.

As the ballet achieved only fourteen performances, only a few pictures are available. The two presented here show the young bride, Ping-Sin, and illustrate in fine detail the period's ideas of how to depict costumes (no. 436) and coiffures (no. 437) in what was considered the 'exotic' style of sixteenth-century China.

436 (c. 1876). Anna Scholl as Ping-Sin (25.10.1875):
'. . . shy Ping-Sin has captured [Prince Yang-Tchoong's] heart at first sight . . .'

437 (1875). Anna Scholl as Ping-Sin, in bridal dress (25.10.1875):
'. . . Yang-Tchoong leads the charming Ping-Sin home as his bride . . .'

Arcona

Ballet in 4 Acts.
Music by Iohan Peter Emilius Hartmann.
Costumes by Edvard Lehmann.
Premiered on May 7, 1875.
Last performance: February 2, 1876.
Number of performances: 14.

In 1874 Copenhagen's old Royal Theatre was demolished to make way for a larger and more modern house. To take full advantage of the new, broader and deeper stage, Bournonville devised a spectacular patriotic ballet, based on meticulous studies of the historic sources dealing with a dramatic episode in the Age of the Valdemars.

Having consolidated the Danish kingdom, Valdemar the Great (see *Waldemar*, nos. 15–60) brought an end to decades of civil war by launching a series of crusades against the Wendish pirates. The most important of these was the crusade of 1168–69, which Bournonville depicted in *Arcona*. This raid aimed at nothing less than the Christianizing of the Slavs of Rügen, and the destruction of Arcona, the fortress and the principal temple of the Slavs containing a colossal figure of their four-headed god, Svantevit.

The critic of *Berlingske Tidende* (May 8, 1875) regretted the lack of strong development in the ballet's plot, which, in itself, was regarded as unfit for a true dramatic purpose. The music, however, was highly praised for its majestic character and melodramatic highlights, such as the scene in Act II with the meeting between Esbern Snare and his bride Hulfried, which is suddenly disrupted by the alarming news of a Wendish invasion. The final battle in the temple of Svantevit (Act IV) was also highly praised, bearing strong reminiscences of Hartmann's previous score for the final battle at Braavalla Heath in *The Valkyrie* (see nos. 381–386).

The photographic records of *Arcona* are rather poor, in spite of the fact that the ballet was premiered with great attention at the beginning of a new era of the rebuilt Royal Theatre, and also at a time when leading dancers were beginning to have photographs of all new rôles taken much more frequently than in previous decades. This lack of photographic documentation can be explained by the very small number of performances given to this somehow unwieldy four-act ballet. Stage pictures, showing Valdemar Gyllich's impressive sceneries, are thus only to be found in two artists' depictions of scenes from Act IV, which were published as woodcut prints in *Illustreret Tidende* (October 19, 1873 and May 16, 1875). The only three photographs available for *Arcona* depict Bishop Absalon's younger brother, Esbern Snare, wearing his wedding clothes in Act II (no. 438), and dressed as a crusader in Act IV (no. 439), while fighting the Slavs of Rügen. No. 440 depicts Esbern Snare's bride, Hulfried, who, disguised as a shield maiden, fights fearlessly at her husband's side.

438 (c. 1875). Waldemar Price as Esbern Snare (7.5.1875); Act II, scene 2:
'. . . Esbern Snare [in wedding dress] comes out onto the landing and is greeted with jubilation . . .'

439 (c. 1875). (cont.) Act IV, scene 9, the battle-scene in the temple of Svantevit:
'. . . The Danes surge forward with irresistible might. Esbern is at their head, and all opposition is crushed . . .'

440 (c. 1875). Betty Schnell as Hulfried (7.5.1875); Act IV, scene 10:
'. . . the banner of the Cross . . . is planted on the base of the [shattered] statue [of the pagan idol Svantevit] by a shield maiden. It is Hulfried, who, unknown to Esbern, has followed the fleet on the Wendish campaign . . .'

From Siberia to Moscow

Ballet in 2 Acts.
Music by Carl Christian Møller.
Costumes by Edvard Lehmann.
Premiered on November 29, 1876.
Last performance: December 4, 1904.
Number of performances: 46.

Having choreographed more than twenty-five 'travelogues', depicting the cultural characteristics of more than fifteen nations within the vast geographic scope from Norway to Italy, and from Argentina via Persia and India to China, it is perhaps not surprising that Bournonville's last ballet was situated in Tsarist Russia.

With the marriage in 1866 of Danish Princess Dagmar to Prince Alexander, later Tsar Alexander III, Denmark became culturally and politically closely bound to Tsarist Russia from the early 1870s throughout the following four decades. It was thus only natural that returning from a six-week visit in 1874 to Saint Petersburg and Moscow, where he was personally received by Princess Dagmar, Bournonville now wanted to mount a ballet set in the picturesque milieu of Tsarist Russia. To give this Russian ballet some spectacular scenic contrasts, the plot was divided into two parts, the first of which was set in a humble room in a log hut in one of the milder places of exile in Siberia, while the second took place in the Great Hall of the Kremlin Imperial Palace of Moscow.

The action traces the cruel fate of a Russian nobleman, Smirnov, who has been exiled to Siberia together with his young daughter Nathalia

(no. 443). A handsome young officer, Ivanov, also exiled to that remote area but recently pardoned, falls in love with the beautiful Nathalia, and together they succeed in escaping from the cruel place of exile by getting the guarding Cossacks drunk with large quantities of vodka during the celebration party for Ivanov's release (nos. 441–442).

Act II takes place at the Imperial Court, where a large number of dances are performed for the Tsar and Tsarina, among which an allegorical divertissement representing the four big European rivers, the Rhône, the Guadalquivir, the Thames and the Rhine, receives particular attention. Suprisingly to all, a fifth river, La Neva, is suddenly represented in dance by Nathalia, who receives so much acclaim for her presentation of this popular Russian national dance that her plea for mercy for her exiled father is granted by the Tsar, and her union with Ivanov is sealed.

The ballet was particularly praised for the lively dance of the Cossacks in Act I, and the divertissement of the four rivers (Act II), of which that of the Thames at once became the most popular with the audience, because of its cheerful and lifelike portrait of two competing English jockeys in a horse race along the river Thames (nos. 444–447).

This divertissement is the only piece of the ballet that has survived to our time, thanks primarily to a film shot by Peter Elfelt in 1905 (see note for no. 444). It was from this film that the dance was reconstructed in 1979 by Niels Bjørn Larsen. Re-entering the repertory of the Royal Danish Ballet in 1980, this dance thus represents the last choreographed, still preserved composition of Bournonville.

441 (1904). Richard Jensen and Gustav Uhlendorff as Cossacks (3.9.1904); Act I, scene 6:
'. . . The invited guests enter [for Ivanov's celebration of being repealed from his Siberian exile] – Tartars and their women as well as [four] Cossacks and their sweethearts gather in a most festive mood . . . amid music, dancing, and merriment . . .'

442 (1904). (cont.) '. . . There are numberless bottles of wine on the [Cossack] leader's table, while kvas and vodka are served as refreshment for the simple folk. Toasts are proposed with cries of jubilation and hurrahs . . .'

443 (c. 1876). Marie Westberg as Nathalia (7.12.1876); Act I, scene 6, *Mazurka*:
'. . . As an invitation to dance, a pleasant surprise is announced, and, together with Ivanov, Nathalia – who is enthusiastically greeted by the whole assembly – performs the very popular mazurka . . .'

444 (1904). Richard Jensen and Gustav Uhlendorff as English jockeys (3.9.1904); Act II, scene 5, *Jockey Dance*:
'. . . [Divertissement representing] THE THAMES in the Horse Race and Reel by two jockeys . . .'

445 (1904). (cont.)

446 (1904). (cont.)

447 (1904). (cont.)

448 (c. 1876). Marie Westberg as Nathalia (7.12.1876); Act II, scene 5, *The Neva*: '. . .[The Hofmarskal] leads before the [Imperial] throne a young Russian girl in white native costume. It is Nathalia, who timidly kneels before Their Majesties . . . Encouraged by the approbation of the imperial couple, her courage and strength begin to mount . . .'

449 (1919). Elna Jørgen-Jensen as Nathalia (4.4.1919); Act II, scene 5, *The Neva*: '. . . and when, swinging her sky blue scarf, she finishes her dance surrounded by a group of river deities and undines, everyone enthusiastically recognises THE RIVER NEVA!. . .'

DIVERTISSEMENTS

La Cracovienne   Polka Militaire

Polish military dance after Fanny Elssler.
Music by Józef Damse and Karol Kurpiński after Polish folktunes, orchestrated by Ambroise Thomas.
Costume adapted from that of the Paris version as designed by Paul Lormier.
Premiered on June 10, 1842.
Last performance: June 19, 1856.
Number of performances: 33.

The great popularity in the nineteenth century of short dances on national themes was encouraged by the phenomenal success of Fanny Elssler's *La Cachucha*, first performed in Jean Coralli's *Le Diable boiteux* in 1836, but frequently danced alone by Elssler and her many imitators. To capitalise on this great success, a similar character pas was introduced for Elssler in Joseph Mazilier's *La Gypsy*, produced at the Paris Opéra on January 28, 1839. This was *La Cracovienne*. Although the ballet is set in Scotland, this traditional Polish dance was performed in full Polish costume. Its fame soon grew to rival the *Cachucha*, and it, too, was imitated by dancers throughout Europe and the United States.

In the spring of 1841 Bournonville visited a number of major European cities including Paris. During this stay he attended the performance of *La Gipsy* on April 23, and on this occasion saw for the first time *La Cracovienne*, which he later described as 'the world's greatest and most famous trifle'. It was then performed by the French ballerina Maria Jacob. With his preparation of a new repertory in mind, Bournonville bought a copy of the *Cracovienne* score, in which he took down the choreography with the clear purpose of bringing it back to Copenhagen. In Copenhagen it was performed from 1842 to 1847 with tremendous success by Caroline Fjeldsted, later followed by Sophie Price (no. 450), who performed in it from 1855 to 1856, after which the solo went out of the repertory.

In 1982 the dance was reconstructed by Knud Arne Jürgensen from Bournonville's 1841 production notes, and staged at the Vienna State Opera on March 31, 1985 as part of a gala performance given in honour of the centenary of Fanny Elssler's death.

450 (c. 1855). Sophie Price (9.11.1855): *La Cracovienne*.

Divertissement.
Music by Hans Christian Lumbye.
Costumes arranged by August Bournonville (since 1862 by Edvard Lehmann).
Premiered on November 1, 1842 (Court Theatre).
Still in repertory.
Number of performances by June 1986: 143.

Polka Militaire plays a significant rôle in the history of the Bournonville family. On December 14, 1798, Bournonville's father Antoine, together with the famous dancer of the time, Margrethe Schall, performed a newly choreographed *Hungarian entré* at Copenhagen's Royal Theatre. This was presented as an incorporated divertissement in Mozart's *The Marriage of Figaro*, given on that day as a charity performance in honour of Antoine's first wife, the dancer Mariane Bournonville, who had tragically died in childbirth in 1797, at the age of only twenty-nine.

This *Hungarian entré*, performed to a lively score by Claus Schall, was restaged on February 18, 1803, in an extended version that included a short overture and two new incorporated dances performed by a small corps de ballet.

In 1814 Antoine Bournonville returned for the last time to this popular divertissement when he arranged two of his original 1798 solos for the 'début' of his promising nine-year-old son, August Bournonville, who performed these Hungarian pas at the Court Theatre in Copenhagen in the summer of 1814.

By the early 1840s the Bohemian polka had become the most popular and widespread social dance of the time, which spurred Bournonville to create a Bohemian-Hungarian divertissement performed by two couples and named *Polka Militaire*. The dance was performed to a newly composed polka score by the Danish Johann Strauss of the time, Hans Christian Lumbye. This divertissement became Bournonville's greatest success within the popular genre of national dance miniatures, and was kept continuously in the repertory until October 11, 1914. In 1949 Harald Lander, with the help of Gustav Uhlendorff, remounted the dance, which from now on was reduced to be performed by only one couple. This version was restaged thirty years later by Hans Brenaa in 1979, and re-entered the repertory of the Royal Danish Ballet on April 22, 1981.

With a choreographic history reaching from 1798 to 1981 this charming Bohemian-Hungarian divertissement can thus be claimed to be the longest living, surviving dance of the Bournonvilles.

The original costumes were made of red *corsages à la hussards* for both sexes, with white skirts for the girls and silvery grey pants for the men, which, when seen together, added an even more sparkling effect to this already most lively national dance.

451 (c. 1883). Charlotte Hansen as Second Lady (12.3.1883): *Polka Militaire*.

452 (1908). Karen Lindahl as First Lady (February 1908): *Polka Militaire*.

453 (1908). (cont.)

454 (1919). Tony Andersen, Aage Eibye, Elna Hansen, John Andersen (4.4.1919): *Polka Militaire*.

Pas des Trois Cousines

Divertissement.
Music by Holger Simon Paulli.
Costumes by Edvard Lehmann.
Premiered on May 20, 1848 (Casino Theatre).
Last performance: January 1, 1970 (Danish Television).
Number of performances (including Casino Theatre and Danish Tele-
vision): 65.

Pas des Trois Cousines became one of Bournonville's most popular and best
known divertissements, perhaps not so much because of the dance itself,
as the 1848 Edvard Lehmann drawing of it (today in the Theatre Museum,
Copenhagen), which was published as a colour lithograph in 1849 and at
once became the most attractive Danish ballet print, the charmer of the
Danish gallery.

In 1847 Bournonville had begun to give private lessons to the talented
children of the Price family – an artistic dynasty of English origin who,
since the beginning of the nineteenth century, had given pantomimes and
small ballet performances during the summer seasons in the private theatres
of Copenhagen. At the direct request of the Prices, Bournonville agreed
in May 1848 to choreograph a pas de trois divertissement for his three most
talented pupils, the cousins Sophie, Juliette, and Amalie Price, of whom
Juliette Price was later to become the personification of Bournonville's ballerina ideal, serving as his prima for fifteen years.

With a beautiful Thorvaldsen-like sculptural effect and a rare purity of
style, the *Pas des Trois Cousines* instantly achieved tremendous success with
the audience, and was included in the repertory of the Royal Danish Ballet
on September 8, 1849, as a result of the engagement of the Price cousins
at the Royal Theatre in that season. Since then the divertissement was performed continuously until 1888, after which it survived only through being
practised at regular intervals in the ballet school. In 1949 Harald Lander
mounted an adapted version of the dance, performed on this occasion to
music taken from *Flower Festival in Genzano* (pas de deux) and *La Sylphide*
(Act I) and pieced together by Emil Reesen. This version was shown on
Danish Television in 1970, but now performed to the original 1848 score
by Holger Simon Paulli. Since then the divertissement has been given only
sporadically on private tours by dancers of the Royal Danish Ballet.

The costumes shown on no. 455 (dating from c. 1885–88) are, in part,
of the original Lehmann design, but with the characteristic attached lace
trimmings that became almost obligatory to the ballet costume in the 1880s.
In no. 456 (dating from 1906), however, the dancers are wearing a refined
version of the obligatory school rehearsal dress as used at that time, probably
because during that period the divertissement was only practised at the
school.

455 (c. 1885–88). Charlotte Hansen (24.11.1885), Elisabeth Soyer (29.11.1885),
Eleonora Monti (understudy for Anna Jensen, 24.11.1885): *Pas des Trois Cousines.*

456 (1906). Olga Hofman, Ellen Tegner, Dagny Brincken (August 1905): *Pas des
Trois Cousines.*

The Prophecy of Love

Seguidilla

Divertissement.
Music by Holger Simon Paulli.
Costumes by Edvard Lehmann.
Premiered on June 4, 1851 (Court Theatre).
Last performance: April 11, 1869.
Number of performances (including Court Theatre): 32.

As is the case with *Pas des Trois Cousines*, this Tyrolean pas de trois divertissement was choreographed at the direct request of the Price cousins Sophie, Juliette and Amalie (see introduction to nos. 455–56).

It was first performed at the Court Theatre at a charity performance given by the Price family, but by September 21, 1851 was included in the repertory of the Royal Theatre, thanks to the extraordinary grace and charm of these three gifted pupils of Bournonville.

The Tyrolean divertissement – a genre that had become popular since the premiere of Rossini's opera *William Tell* at the Paris Opéra in 1829 – depicts, according to Bournonville's memoirs: 'A Tyrolean scene with a changing dance that takes place between three young maidens who consult the oracles of the flowers, the knitting, and the cards about their affaires of the heart.'

On September 4, 1857 Petrine Fredstrup (no. 457) took over the part from Amalie Price, who had left the theatre after her marriage the same year. Because of its great popularity, the divertissement was restaged on February 28, 1869 in an extended version that included the three suitors of the young maidens, and as a result of this the original changing dance was transformed into a large-scale Tyrolean pas des six.

Divertissement.
Music by Holger Simon Paulli.
Costumes by Edvard Lehmann.
Premiered on September 1, 1868.
Last performance: December 21, 1869.
Number of performances: 12.

The *Seguidilla*, Bournonville's last dance in the Spanish genre, was choreographed especially for the two leading dancers of the Royal Danish Ballet during the 1860s and '70s, Betty Schnell and Anna Scholl, serving as a display vehicle for their individual talents.

It was presented on the playbill as 'A changing dance in Spanish style', and consisted of a series of tiny variations for each girl, alternating with each other in a sort of non-stop choreographic contest and ending in a roguish joint Finale. At each alternation between the girls they performed a few steps together while encircling each other *dos à dos*: this moment can be glimpsed on photographs nos. 460–61. Although the dance was very popular, and was extensively performed for two full seasons, it had a strong competitor in the no less popular *Seguidilla* from *La Ventana* (see introduction to that ballet), which had been given as an independent divertissement since October 21, 1866, and thus soon manoeuvred the 1868 *Seguidilla* out of the repertory.

457 (c. 1861). Petrine Fredstrup (4.9.1857): *The prophecy of Love*.

458 (c. 1868-71). Betty Schnell (1.9.1868): *Seguidilla*.

459 (1870). Anna Scholl (1.9.1868): *Seguidilla.*

460 (1870). Betty Schnell and Anna Scholl (1.9.1868): *Seguidilla.*

461 (c. 1871–73). (cont.)

OPERAS

Brahma and the Bayadère

(Le Dieu et la Bayadère, ou La Courtisane amoureuse)

Opera-Ballet in 2 Acts.
Book by Eugène Scribe.
Music by Daniel-François-Ésprit Auber.
Costumes by Johan Christian Ryge adapted from the Paris version as designed by Hippolyte Lecomte.
Premiered on May 28, 1833; mise-en-scène by August Bournonville since February 2, 1841.
Last performance: January 12, 1873 (Act I performed separately on June 3, 1873).
Number of performances: 66.

Auber's opera was originally written for the Paris Opéra and premiered there on October 13, 1830 with choreography by Filippo Taglioni, devised especially for his daughter Marie Taglioni. The opera seemed to suit perfectly her unique qualities, and became a tremendous success, thanks in great part to her performance of the rôle of the dancing bayadère, Zoloé, of whom the Brahma and an Indian prince are both enamoured, the former in the disguise of a man of low rank at the court of the latter. In Act I the disguised Brahma succeeds in winning Zoloé's affection and, after testing her devotion by submitting for a while to the resentment of his rival, and by a pretended caprice in favour of a singing bayadère, Ninka, who accompanies her, he marries Zoloé, and saves her from the flames (Act II), as she is about to be burned for marrying beneath her caste.

In Copenhagen the opera was first staged with choreography by Paul Funck, for many years a prominent dancer and respected teacher at the ballet school of the Royal Theatre. In 1841 Bournonville took over the staging in co-operation with dancer Pierre Larcher, devising new choreography that was closer to Taglioni's original version, which Lucile Grahn had introduced to Copenhagen in 1837.

On October 10, 1859 Bournonville restaged the opera in a new version for Juliette Price, who was replaced in 1871 by Marie Westberg (nos. 462–63), a Swedish dancer who spent most of her career in Copenhagen. On that occasion Westberg was joined by Bournonville's daughter, the singer Charlotte Bournonville, who performed the rôle of Ninka. Among the opera's many dances the *Pas du châle* in Act I (no. 463) stood out as a true highlight, acclaimed for its aesthetic effects, created by the numerous pink scarfs which floated and hovered in the air in the most ingenious combinations.

The two photographs (both from 1871) with Marie Westberg performing as Zoloé show how little the romantic ballerina costume had changed since the opera's 1830 premiere. On a French print dating from the early 1830s it appears as nearly identical with the costume of the 1871 Danish production. It represents a classic example of the silver-white bell-shaped ballerina costume that came so strongly into fashion with the creation of *La Sylphide* in 1832, but had already been anticipated in 1830 in *Le Dieu et la Bayadère*.

462 (c. 1871–73). Marie Westberg as Zoloé (8.10.1871); Act I, scene 2:
'. . . At this moment the sounds of the songs and the tambourines become increasingly louder; Bayadères exit from the pagoda . . . Zoloé is leading the *dancing bayadères* . . .' (*Det kongelige Theaters Repertoire* nr. 93, p.2)

463 (c. 1871–73). (cont.) Act I, scene 5, *Pas du châle*:
'. . . All the bayadères are fighting for the shawls in the coffins; they tear them from each other and toss them around themselves. They form numerous groups with Zoloé while surrounding her. The unknown person [the Bramah in disguise], who is sitting on a stone, goes into raptures by gazing at them . . .' (*idem*, p.4)

The Mute Girl of Portici

(*La Muette de Portici*)

Opera in 5 Acts.
Book by Eugène Scribe and Casimir Delavigne.
Music by Daniel-François-Ésprit Auber.
Scenery by Arnold Wallich.
Costumes by Johan Christian Ryge partly adapted from older repertory (since 1862 by Edvard Lehmann).
Premiered on May 22, 1930; mise-en-scène by August Bournonville since October 22, 1847.
Last performance: September 15, 1915.
Number of performances: 196.

La Muette de Portici was given its Copenhagen premiere during Bournonville's first season as newly appointed ballet-master. On that occasion the demanding mime rôle of Fenella was given to the young leading Danish actress of the time, Johanne Louise Heiberg. This aroused Bournonville's strong indignation at not having been asked to instruct one of his leading ballerinas in this important part, as had been the tradition in this opera since the rôle was created by French ballerina Lise Noblet at the Paris Opéra on February 28, 1828.

In spite of Bournonville's consistent refusals to assist Heiberg with her preparations for the many demanding mime scenes, she created a real stir with her highly personal interpretation of the mute Fenella, thanks both to her refined dramatic talent and to her previous years as a student at the ballet school. This remarkable success made her comment later, a little maliciously, in her memoirs, that when Bournonville himself taught the rôle in 1847 to dancer Caroline Fjeldsted, the rôle by then was nothing more than 'a laterally reversed copy of my own original interpretation'. However, with Bournonville's *mise-en-scène* the opera became even more popular with the audience, and was kept in repertory for another seventy years.

The dances included a pas de deux and a *Bolero* in Act I, while Act III was enlivened by a *Tarantella*. The most popular of these was the Act I pas de deux, which was originally based on a piece by the French dancer François Décombe (known as Albert), whom Bournonville had known and admired during his sojourn in Paris in the late 1820s. In 1873 this pas de deux was replaced by a new extended version that included six (later eight) ladies around the leading couple, and was performed to a score arranged by Vilhelm Christian Holm. This extended 1873 divertissement was incorporated in Act II of *The Kermesse in Brüges* on November 7, 1909, and has ever since been performed in that ballet as a divertissement at Mme van Everdingen's.

The photographs available nearly all focus on the character of Fenella and in particular the long mime scene in Act IV (nos. 468–70) where she describes her fear and desperation at the turmoil and destruction that has fallen upon the city of Naples as a result of the revolution headed by her brother Masaniello (nos. 466, 471). This scene was regarded as a touchstone for any mimic dancer in the last century. It was brilliantly performed by Laura Stillmann for nearly twenty years, after which she herself instructed all the succeeding dancers in the rôle up to the opera's last production in 1913. The part of Fenella thus represents a fine example of the strong mimic continuity in the Bournonville tradition. The Act IV scene with Fenella – a part which had also been brilliantly performed by Fanny Elssler – was reconstructed from Bournonville's production notes by Knud Arne Jürgensen in 1985, and staged at the Vienna State Opera on March 31 the same year, as part of the gala performance given in honour of the centenary of Elssler's death.

464 (1913). Act III, second set: '. . . Naples. The big marketplace. A fair is going on. The square is filled with street shops . . . a *Tarantella* is performed . . .' (*Det kongelige Theaters Repertoire*, nr. 26, p.7)

465 (1864). Laura Stillmann as Fenella (13.10.1850); Act III, second set:
'. . . The fishergirls, and among them is Fenella, arrive with their fruit and flower
baskets on their heads [and] sit down in the front of the stage with Fenella in their
midst. She is sorrowful and pensive and takes no part in what happens around her
. . .' (*idem*, p.7)

466 (1864). Jens Larsen Nyrop as Masaniello (12.2.1862); Act III, second set:
'. . . Salva [the viceroy's officer] and his soldiers are just about to abduct Fenella
when Masaniello and some fishermen suddenly appear at the marketplace . . . and
draw their weapons. In a moment Salva and his soldiers are disarmed and put to
flight . . .' (*idem*, p.8)

467 (1913). Act IV (since 1875 same set as in Act II): '. . . The outskirts of Portici. [To the left] Masaniello's cottage. At both
sides, cliffs, in the background, the sea. Daybreak . . .' (*idem*, p.8)

468 (c. 1869–77). Laura Stillmann as Fenella (13.10.1850); Act IV:
'. . . Fenella arrives exhausted and staggering: "This horrific state in which Naples finds itself! Imagine the horror and terror now fallen upon the city! Plunder, murder, and conflagration everywhere!" . . . (*idem*, p. 9)

469 (1886). Anna Jensen as Fenella (26.4.1886); Act IV:
'. . . [Fenella:] "I am exhausted and need to rest!" . . .' (*idem*, p.9)

470 (1913). Elna Jørgen-Jensen as Fenella (5.10.1913) and Vilhelm Herold as Masaniello (5.10.1913); Act IV:
'. . . She takes a seat at the bench [next to Masaniello] and falls into a deep sleep [listening to his comforting aria] . . .' (*idem*, p.9)

471 (1864). Jens Larsen Nyrop as Masaniello (12.2.1862) and Laura Stillmann as Fenella (13.10.1850); Act IV, Finale:
'. . . Masaniello is presented with the keys of Naples. He is dressed in a magnificent mantle . . . Fenella who is next to her brother moves her eyes toward the sky and seems to pray for him . . .' (*idem*, p.11)

The Troubadour

Opera in 4 Acts.
Book by Salvatore Cammarano.
Music by Giuseppe Verdi.
Scenery by Christian Ferdinand Christensen.
Costumes by Edvard Lehmann.
Premiered on September 10, 1865.
Last performance (the ballet divertissement performed separately): January 22, 1926.
Number of performances (including the ballet divertissement performed separately): 201.

The Troubadour was the only Verdi opera to be produced at Copenhagen's Royal Theatre in Bournonville's lifetime. Premiered at the Paris Opéra on January 12, 1857, with a ballet divertissement at the opening of Act III choreographed by Lucien Petipa, the Paris version became the model for Bournonville's production with regard to the overall choreographic structure and casting of the divertissement, which was performed in both Paris and Copenhagen by a leading couple, three gipsy girls, and a corps de ballet. The score for Bournonville's version, however, was completely different from that of the Paris production, being an arrangement by Danish com-poser Axel Grandjean of a number of melodies from the opera's second act, set together with a newly composed Finale galop by Hans Christian Lumbye.

The divertissement was instantly well received, and was performed as an independent ballet from January 25, 1867, thereby later becoming Bournonville's most often performed opera divertissement.

On October 10, 1941, *The Troubadour* was restaged with a new divertissement, choreographed by Børge Ralov with the assistance of the then long retired ballerina Valborg Borchsenius, who had performed in the opera's ballet divertissement from 1892 to 1908. Ralov's choreography, however, was only in very small parts based on Bournonville's original version, and was performed to a completely new score of various Verdi fragments pieced together by conductor Egisto Tango.

The *Troubadour* photographs presented here are particularly interesting in that they show in fine detail the many subtle changes of the ballet costumes that took place between 1865 and 1912. Lehmann's original costumes (no. 473), which are among his most beautiful designs, were adapted by his successors Pietro Krohn, 1885 (no. 474), Vilhelm Rosenstand, 1899 (no. 475), and Vilhelm Tetens, 1912 (no. 476), all adding a number of small but significant alterations to Lehmann's original design.

472 (1902?). Act III, scenes 1–4: '. . . A camp of tents. To the right, the tent of count Luna, from which a banner is flying. In the background, the castle of Castellor . . .' (*Det kongelige Theaters Repertoire*, nr. 190, p.8)

473 (c. 1876). Charlotte Schousgaard (3.11.1875) and Athalia Flammé (7.1.1876) as two (out of three) leading gipsy ladies; Act III, scene 1, *The gipsy dance*.

474 (c. 1885). Athalia Reumert as the leading gipsy lady (1.5.1885); Act III, scene 1, *The gipsy dance*.

475 (1906). Valborg Guldbrandsen as the leading gipsy lady (14.1.1892); Act III, scene 1, *The gipsy dance*.

476 (1913). Ketty Huldstrøm (15.9.1912), Holger Mehnen (15.9.1912) and Wanda Mathiesen (15.9.1912) as three gipsies of the corps de ballet; Act III, scene 1, *The gipsy dance*.

William Tell

Opera in 4 Acts.
Book by Victor Joseph Étienne de Jouy and Hippolyte Louis Florent Bis.
Music by Gioacchino Rossini.
Scenery by Christian Ferdinand Christensen (since 1873 by Valdemar Gyllich).
Costumes (since 1873) by Edvard Lehmann.
Premiered on September 4, 1842; mise-en-scène by August Bournonville since November 16, 1873.
Last performance: December 10, 1921.
Number of performances: 111.

William Tell was premiered at the Paris Opéra on August 3, 1829. The action depicts the liberation of the Swiss cantons from the Austrian yoke, through the patriotism of the bold mountaineer William Tell, who has long cherished the hope of freeing his countrymen from the tyranny of the Austrians as personified by the stern and cruel Governor Gesler.

The opera's dance divertissement, the centrepiece of which is a Tyrolean pas de trois, was performed at the opening of the second scene of Act III, and takes place at a festival, in which Gesler orders the people to bow before his hat, hoisted up on a pole (no. 477).

Bournonville, who was present at the opera's 1829 Paris premiere, found the plot too lengthy to be staged in Copenhagen, which may explain why he did not choreograph the divertissement for the first production of the opera in Copenhagen on September 4, 1842. On that occasion the divertissement was choreographed by French dancer François Lefèbvre, who was engaged as dancer and choreographer at the Royal Danish Ballet from 1842 to 1847.

Lefèbvre's production was kept unchanged until 1873, when Bournonville choreographed a new Tyrolean pas de trois, which was later restaged in an extended version by his successor Emil Hansen, who added a corps de ballet section to Bournonville's divertissement on February 5, 1889. In 1926 Gustav Uhlendorff choreographed a new version: by then the opera had been out of the repertory for exactly thirty years. This version, which bears very little resemblance to Bournonville's original choreography, formed the basis for a new divertissement, rechoreographed fifty-four years later by Hans Brenaa on May 10, 1980 and still performed by the Royal Danish Ballet as an independent divertissement.

477 (1921). Act III, scene 2: '. . . The marketplace in Altorf decorated for festivities with a platform for the bailiff [Gesler] and his suite on stage right. Just opposite this is erected a pole on top of which the hat of Gesler is fixed. To both sides, appletrees and limetrees . . .' (*Det kongelige Theaters Repertoire*, nr. 144, p. 10)

478 (c. 1875). Anna Scholl (21.11.1875); Act III, scene 2, *Pas de trois*:
'. . . The festivities begin. Among the various dancers are also a number of Tyroleans, among whom a girl distinguishes herself by her light dancing to the accompaniment of a Tyrolean song . . .' (*idem*, p.10)

List of Pictures

Each photograph is registered with (a) name of photographer(s), (b) dating of the photograph, (c) description of photograph, (d) present location of original.

ABBREVIATIONS

neg.: Glass plate negative (16.5 × 12 cm if not otherwise indicated).
All glass plate negatives taken by Holger Damgaard are in size 15 × 9.9 cm except nos. 181–182 & 190–192, which are in size 11.9 × 8.9 cm.

C. de v.: Carte-de-visite photograph (standard size: 8.2 × 5.5 cm, mounted on carton 10 × 6.3 cm).★

C.c.: Cabinet card photograph (standard size: 14 × 10.3 cm, mounted on carton 16.6 × 10.7 cm).★

P.s.: Postcard size (13.8 × 8.9 cm if not otherwise indicated).

DKKk: Royal Library (*Billedsamlingen*), Christians Brygge 8, DK–1219 Copenhagen K.

DKKt: The Theatre Museum (*Teatermuseet*), Christiansborg Ridebane 10, DK–1218 Copenhagen K.

DKKkt: The Royal Theatre (*Det kongelige Teaters bibliotek og arkiv*), Tordenskjoldsgade 3, DK–1055 Copenhagen K.

★Small variations from the Carte-de-visite and Cabinet card standard sizes do occur.

1. Harald Paetz, 1868; C. de v.; DKKt.
2. Sofus Peter Christensen and E. L. & L. J. Morange, taken between October 27 and November 11, 1886; C. de v.; DKKk.
3. Theodor Collin, c. 1861–62 (outdoor shot); C. de v.; DKKt.
4. Bertel Christian Budtz Müller & Co., taken between February 1875 and March 1876; C. de v.; DKKk.
5. Sofus Peter Christensen and E. L. & L. J. Morange, taken between October 27 and November 11, 1886; C.c.; DKKk.
6. Same as no. 1.
7. Same as no. 5.
8. Same as no. 1.
9. Sofus Peter Christensen and E. L. & L. J. Morange, taken between November 11, 1886 and March 1887; C.c.; DKKt.
10. Sofus Peter Christensen and E. L. & L. J. Morange, taken between October 27 and November 11, 1886; C. de v.; DKKt.
11. Same as no. 10.
12. Same as no. 1.
13. Unknown photographer, taken between December 8, 1849 and November 1855; C. de v.; DKKt.
14. Theodor Collin, c. 1861–62 (outdoor shot); C. de v.; DKKt.
15. Unknown photographer, taken for the production December 8, 1901; photograph (11.5 × 17.3 cm) mounted in *Maskinmesterprotokol XXXII, serie 2 (1904)*; DKKkt.
Scenery originally by Arnold Wallich (1835). Completely repainted by Valdemar Gyllich in 1871 and again in 1877 with minor alterations in order to fit the dimensions of the new theatre. New scenery again by Valdemar Gyllich (1893). Repainted by Thorolf Pedersen (1901) with only minor alterations (seen here). In use until 1920.
16. Peter Elfelt, September 1909; neg. (plate no. 5911); DKKk.
17. Georg Lindström, December 1901; unmounted photograph (16.6 × 9.6 cm); E. Freddie collection.
18. Peter Elfelt, May 1907; neg. (plate no. 4726); DKKk.
19. Peter Newland, October 1920; C.c.; E. Merrild collection.
20. Harald Paetz, taken between 1870 and September 16, 1872; C. de v.; DKKk.
21. Theodor Collin, 1861 (outdoor shot); C. de v.; DKKt.
22. Harald Paetz, c. 1870; C. de v.; DKKt.
23. Georg Lindström, taken in January or February 1901; P.s.; DKKk.
This photograph was first published in *Teatret*, February 1902, *4. Hefte*, (p. 73). Later it was printed as a postcard.
24. Jens Petersen & Søn, June 1881; photomontage (12.8 × 17.5 cm) mounted on carton (23.1 × 27.6 cm). DKKk.
In the years 1881–83 August Westrup and Ernst Bojesen published twelve stage pictures entitled *Minder fra Theaterverdenen* (Theatre souvenirs) which included popular scenes from the Royal Theatre's repertory. *Waldemar* was no. 3 in this series. The scenery depicted here is by Valdemar Gyllich and dates back to the production on September 13, 1871. It was in use until February 14, 1874. Only the six foreground figures in this montage are photographs, the rest are painted.
25. Unknown photographer, taken for the production December 8, 1901; photograph (11.5 × 17.3 cm) mounted in *Maskinmesterprotokol, serie 2 (1904)*; DKKkt.
Scenery originally by Troels Lund (1835). In 1874 Valdemar Gyllich painted new scenery for Act II of I. P. E. Hartmann's 1846 opera *Liden Kirsten*, when it was restaged for the inaugural performance of the new Royal Theatre on October 11, 1874. From June 1, 1877 this set also served as the décor for Act II of *Waldemar*. In use until 1920.

26. Marie Budtz & Co., taken between January 29 and December 8, 1893; C.c.; DKKk.
27. Peter Elfelt, April 1907; neg. (plate no. 4643); DKKk.
28. [Georg Rosenkilde], taken between November 1866 and autumn 1871; C.c. (with frame of flower ornaments); DKKk.
29. Georg Rosenkilde, taken between November 1866 and autumn 1871; C. de v.; DKKt.
30. N. C. Hansen and F. C. L. Weller, taken between 1877 and October 1885; C.c.; DKKk.
31. Emil Hohlenberg, taken between February 1893 and April 2, 1894; C. de v.; DKKt.
32. Peter Elfelt, May 1907; neg. (plate no. 4642); DKKk.
33. Peter Elfelt, May 1904; neg. (plate no. 3395); DKKk.
34. Peter Elfelt, April 1907; neg. (plate no. 4622); DKKk.
35. Peter Elfelt, April 1907; neg. (plate no. 4620); DKKk.
36. Peter Elfelt, April 1907; neg. (plate no. 4623); DKKk.
37. Peter Elfelt, April 1907; neg. (plate no. 4624); DKKk.
38. Peter Elfelt, April 1907; neg. (plate no. 4625); DKKk.
39. Peter Newland, October 1920; C.c.; E. Merrild collection.
40. Peter Elfelt, April 1907; neg. (plate no. 4631); DKKk.
41. Emil Hohlenberg, taken between February 1893 and April 2, 1894; C. de v.; DKKt.
42. Peter Elfelt, May 1904; neg. (plate no. 3396); DKKk.
43. Unknown photographer, October 1920; unmounted photograph (16.7 × 11.1 cm); DKKkt.
44. Peter Elfelt, April 1907; neg. (plate no. 4628); DKKk.
45. Peter Elfelt, April 1907; neg. (plate no. 4637); DKKk.
46. Peter Elfelt, May 1904; neg. (plate no. 3397); DKKk.
47. Marie Budtz & Co., taken between January and December 8, 1893; C.c.; DKKt.
48. Unknown photographer, taken for the production December 12, 1901; photograph (11.5 × 17.3 cm) mounted in *Maskinmesterprotokol XXXII serie 2* (1904); DKKkt.
The scenery of Act IV consisted originally of three sets:
1. Waldemar's tent (painted by Arnold Wallich).
2. 'Denmark's Future, an apotheosis' (tableau painted by Troels Lund).
3. Grathe Heath (painted by C. F. Christensen).
The first of these depicted the interior of Waldemar's tent and is described in the original programme as: 'Waldemar's tent. A couch-bed [to the right] shaded by banners and a table upon which are a lamp and Waldemar's weapons'. This set had a transparent back-cloth through which a series of *tableaux vivants* were seen, representing Waldemar's dream 'Denmark's Future! Moments from six centuries' (Act IV, second set). The third set showed Grathe Heath, where the famous battle between the armies of Svend and Waldemar took place on October 23, 1157, and in which the latter's triumph marked the start of an era known as the Age of the Waldemars.
After the production on January 29, 1893, the entire scene with Waldemar's dream was omitted and the first two sets abandoned. Instead, Waldemar's tent was now added to the Grathe Heath scenery, which from then on was the only décor used in Act IV. This set (seen here) was adapted by Thorolf Pedersen. In use until May 5, 1907. For the ballet's last staging on October 10, 1920, Thorolf Pedersen painted new scenery for Act IV (see nos. 51 and 60). This was in use until December 26, 1920, when the ballet was given its last performance.
49. Marie Budtz & Co., taken between January and December 8, 1893; C.c.; DKKk.
This photograph is a fine example of how the photographer has attempted

to create a true stage illusion in the studio, here depicting the brewing storm at the battlefield on Grathe Heath.

50. Unknown photographer, taken October 1920; unmounted photograph (21.5 × 14.1 cm); DKKkt.
51. Sophus Juncker-Jensen, October 1920; unmounted, photograph (10.5 × 22.5 cm); DKKkt.
    Photograph taken on the stage of the Royal Theatre for the production on October 10, 1920. Scenery by Thorolf Pedersen (1920). In use until December 26, 1920.
52. Harald Paetz, c. 1870; C. de v.; DKKk.
53. Peter Elfelt, April 1907; neg. (plate no. 4638); DKKk.
54. Peter Elfelt, April 1907; neg. (plate no. 4626); DKKk.
55. Peter Elfelt, May 1904; neg. (plate no. 3398); DKKk.
56. Emil Hohlenberg, taken between February 1893 and April 2, 1894; C. de v.; DKKk.
57. Harald Paetz, c. 1871; C. de v.; DKKt.
58. Emil Hohlenberg, taken between February 1893 and April 2, 1894; C.c.; DKKt.
59. Emil Hohlenberg, taken between February 1893 and April 2, 1894; C. de v.; DKKt.
60. Same as no. 51.
61. Unknown photographer, taken for the production November 11, 1917 or earlier (1903?); photograph (12.9 × 17.9 cm) mounted in *Maskinmesterprotokol 25, serie 1* (1917–18); DKKkt.
    Scenery originally arranged by Arnold Wallich (1836) with use of older sets and props. Repainted with only minor alterations by Valdemar Gyllich (1882) in order to fit the dimensions of the new theatre. Kept without any changes until 1923, when Thorolf Pedersen added ceiling chandelier and wall carpets. In use until 1924.
62. Georg Lindström, September 1903, C.c.; DKKt.
    This photograph is the first in a series of thirty known pictures, of which twenty-six were taken in Lindström's studio in Købmagergade 42, while the remaining four were taken on the stage of the Royal Theatre. Four photographs from this series were first published in *Teatret, 8. Hefte, II Aargang* (September 1903) pp. 118–20, while twenty-one photographs were presented in *Hver 8. Dag*, no. 13 (December 25), 1904. The complete series was sold as cabinet card photographs and, in selection, as postcards. The Theatre Museum owns eighteen photographs of the series, which represents one of the most important single sources to this ballet.
63. Harald Paetz, 1866; C. de v.; DKKk.
    Juliette Price performed this rôle for the last time on November 15, 1859. The photograph was thus taken as a souvenir seven years later, when she had retired from the stage owing to a serious injury.
64. Peter Elfelt, August 28, 1905; neg. (plate no. 3725); DKKk.
    This and the following two photographs are enlargements of frames from a film (30 metres) originally shot by Elfelt in his studio at Købmagergade 64 in October, 1903 (Elfelt moving picture negative no. 68).
65. Peter Elfelt, August 28, 1905; neg. (plate no. 3727); DKKk.
66. Peter Elfelt, August 28, 1905; neg. (plate no. 3726); DKKk.
67. Same as no. 62.
68. Same as no. 62.
69. Same as no. 62.
70. Peter Newland, May 1918; unmounted photograph (15.8 × 11.7 cm); E. Merrild collection.
    Showcase photograph taken for a summer tour in the Danish provinces 1918, arranged and directed by Karl Merrild with eleven dancers of the Royal Danish Ballet.
71. Harry Paetz, 1895; C.c.; DKKt.
72. Georg Lindström, September 1903; photograph (11.4 × 17 cm) published in *Teatret* (September, 1903), *8. Hefte, II Aargang*, p. 120; DKKk.
73. Georg Lindström, September 1903; P.s.; DKKk.
74. Same as no. 70.
    Note the rôle of John (James's father) created especially for Merrild's 1918 summer tour instead of the original rôle of Anna (James's mother).
75. Harald Paetz, September 1871; C. de v.; DKKt.
    In this picture, showing Westberg in her first part, the photographer has attempted to create an actual stage illusion, when the Sylphide appears in the window. Note the rather heavy flower-garland and the flowing hair, an appearance essentially different from that of Marie Taglioni in Paris 1832.
76. Same as no. 62.
77. Same as no. 62.
78. Same as no. 62.
79. Same as no. 62.
80. Same as no. 62.

81. Same as no. 62.
82. Peter Elfelt, January 1909; neg. (plate no. 5689); DKKk.
    In the original 1836 version the two male solos in Act I (today known as Gurn's and James's solos) were performed by two young Scottish peasants. Not before April 11, 1934 were these solos actually performed by Gurn and James. Note the classic low arm position (*bras bas*), a trademark of Bournonville's school. With the characteristic rounded hands, here perfectly demonstrated by Merrild, this arm position represents one of the basic elements of the Bournonville style.
83. Peter Elfelt, January 1909; neg. (plate no. 5697); DKKk.
84. Same as no. 62.
85. Same as no. 62.
86. Unknown photographer, taken for the production November 11, 1917 or earlier (1903?); photograph (12.9 × 17.9 cm) mounted in *Maskinmesterprotokol 25, serie 1* (1917–18); DKKkt.
    Scenery originally by Arnold Wallich (1836). Rearranged by Valdemar Gyllich (1882) with use of older sets in order to fit the dimensions of the new theatre. In use until 1924. The original scenery (1836–71) had a floor carpet with painted grass and earth. Note the loom at centre stage on which the witch Madge weaves the poisonous scarf, a scene omitted since the production on April 13, 1939.
87. Peter Fristrup, taken between February 1882 and 1883; C. de v.; DKKk.
88. Sophus Juncker-Jensen, 1913; P.s. (coloured); DKKk.
89. Same as no. 62.
90. Peter Fristrup, taken between February 1882 and 1883; C.c.; DKKk.
91. Leopold Hartmann, 1882; C.c.; DKKt.
    Note the dancer's staffs of support (here clearly retouched). Because of the long exposure time (in the 1880s about ten seconds) these staffs were needed when more difficult attitudes and balances were shot.
92. Peter Elfelt, April 1908; C.c. (plate no. 5207); DKKt.
93. Georg Lindström, September 1903; photograph (12.8 × 22.8 cm) mounted on carton (15.5 × 24 cm); K. A. Jürgensen collection.
    This stage picture was the only one of the series from *La Sylphide* taken by Lindström in 1903 to be printed in large format (see note for no. 62). Later it was also printed as a postcard.
94. Same as no. 70.
95. Georg Lindström, September 1903; C.c.; E. Beck collection.
96. Peter Elfelt, September 23, 1905; neg. (plate no. 3889); DKKk.
97. Unknown photographer, c. September 1871; C.c.; DKKt.
98. Sofus Peter Christensen and E. L. & L. J. Morange, taken between November 1892 and November 1895; C.c.; DKKt.
99. Leopold Hartmann, c. 1882; photomontage (12.7 × 17.6 cm) mounted on carton (23.1 × 27.6 cm); DKKk.
    This picture appears as no. 8 in the album *Minder fra Theaterverdenen*, published 1881–83 by August Westrup and Ernst Bojesen (see note for no. 24). The scenery depicted here is by Valdemar Gyllich and dates back to the production of February 5, 1882.
100. Same as no. 62.
101. Same as no. 62.
102. Same as no. 73.
103. Harald Paetz, September 1871; C. de v.; DKKt.
104. Same as no. 62.
105. Same as no. 73.
106. Unknown photographer, taken for the production May 14, 1919; photograph (12.8 × 17.3 cm) mounted in *Maskinmesterprotokol 26, serie 1*; DKKkt.
    Scenery originally by C. F. Christensen (1839). Rearranged by Valdemar Gyllich (1882) with use of older sets from Oehlenschläger's drama *Corregio* (restaged at the new theatre on September 1, 1877). In use until 1919. Parts of this scenery were also used in the production of Mascagni's opera *Cavalleria rusticana*, premiered on September 30, 1891.
107. Unknown photographer, taken for the production May 14, 1919; unmounted photograph (22.9 × 16.2 cm); DKKkt.
108. Peter Newland, May 1919; C.c.; E. Merrild collection.
109. Emil Hohlenberg, taken between December 1882 and May 1883; C.c.; DKKt.
110. Unknown photographer, taken for the production March 22, 1929; neg. DKKkt.
    Scenery by Ove Christian Pedersen (1929). In use until December 8, 1929. The original scenery by C. F. Christensen (1840) consisted of only one set (see captions to nos. 110 and 127). For Elna Jørgen-Jensen's restaging of the ballet in 1929 the décor was divided into two sets in order to fit better with the large number of new Spanish dances incorporated by Elna Jørgen-Jensen and Harald Lander in this production. In an oil painting by Edvard Lehmann (painted in 1840 and showing Augusta Nielsen as Céleste performing the 'Je suis la bayadère' solo of Act I) a small glimpse of Christensen's original scenery can be seen. This painting is today in the Theatre Museum.

111. Christian Reinau, c. 1905; C.c.; M. Castenskiold collection.
112. Emil Rye & Co., taken between May 1881 and 1887; C. de v.; DKKt.
113. Sofus Peter Christensen and E. L. & L. J. Morange, c. 1884; C.c.; DKKk.
114. Peter Elfelt, May 1911; neg. (24 × 18 cm; plate no. 6755); DKKk. Photograph taken in the dance studio at the Royal Theatre.
115. Holger Damgaard, taken for the production March 22, 1929; unmounted photograph (22.8 × 15.1 cm); DKKkt. Photograph taken on the stage of the Royal Theatre. Décor by Ove Christian Pedersen.
116. Frederik Schmidt and Rasmus Malling, taken between March 1864 and November 1870; C. de v.; DKKt.
117. Emil Hohlenberg, taken between May 1881 and September 1882; C. de v.; DKKk.
118. Sophus Juncker-Jensen, 1899; C.c.; DKKt.
119. Peter Elfelt, 1911; neg. (plate no. 6743); DKKk.
120. Peter Elfelt, May 1904; neg. (plate no. 3405); DKKk.
121. Peter Elfelt, June 1911; neg. (plate no. 6771); DKKk.
122. Theodor Collin, c. 1861–62 (outdoor shot); C. de v.; DKKt.
123. Peter Elfelt, May 1904; neg. (plate no. 3406); DKKk.
124. Emil Hohlenberg, June 1889; C. de v.; DKKt. Photograph taken for the farewell performance of Anna Tychsen on June 3, 1889.
125. Peter Elfelt, June 1911; neg. (plate no. 6779); DKKk. Note the classic Bournonville *arabesque penchée* in this picture, with the stretched left arm held parallel with the lifted left leg and the eyes fixed on the right hand as it goes downwards during the see-sawing *penché* movement – all perfectly demonstrated here by Grethe Ditlevsen. Céleste's 'Je suis la bayadère' solo in Act I was performed to the famous violin solo *Polonaise* by Joseph Mayseder.
126. Peter Elfelt, May 1904; neg. (plate no. 3401); DKKk.
127. Unknown photographer, taken for the production March 22, 1929; neg.; DKKkt. Scenery by Ove Christian Pedersen (1929). In use until December 8, 1929. See also note for no. 110.
128. Peter Elfelt, May 1911; neg. (24 × 18 cm; plate no. 6757); DKKk. Photograph taken in the dance studio of the Royal Theatre.
129. Sophus Juncker-Jensen, 1899; C.c.; DKKt.
130. Peter Elfelt, May 1911; neg. (24 × 18 cm; plate no. 6756); DKKk. Photograph taken in the dance studio of the Royal Theatre.
131. Peter Elfelt, June 1911; neg. (plate no. 6772); DKKk.
132. Theodor Collin, c. 1861–62 (outdoor shot); C. de v.; DKKt.
133. Leopold Hartmann, taken between May 1881 and August 7, 1882; C.c.; DKKk.
134. Peter Elfelt, May 1909; neg. (plate no. 5848); DKKk. Nos. 134–136 are showcase photographs taken for a summer tour to Berlin in 1909. The four dancers depicted performed on this tour as an independent group named *De fire* (The four).
135. Peter Elfelt, May 1909; neg. (plate no. 5846); DKKk.
136. Peter Elfelt, May 1909; neg. (plate no. 5834); DKKk.
137. Unknown photographer, taken for the production March 15, 1914 or earlier (1903?); unmounted photograph (12.9 × 17.9 cm); DKKkt. Scenery originally by C. F. Christensen (1842). Repainted by Valdemar Gyllich (1875) with only minor alterations in order to fit the dimensions of the new theatre. Rearranged by Thorolf Pedersen (1898) with use of older sets and props from Auber's opera *La Muette de Portici*. In use until 1923.
138. Theodor Collin, March 29, 1862 (outdoor shot); C. de v.; DKKkt. Note the dancer's staff of support, used because of the long exposure time. On this photograph it is clearly visible although most photographers of the time tried to have it hidden by the dancer's posing. In later years, when the photographic art became more refined, these staffs were normally touched out.
139. Sophus Juncker-Jensen, 1922; unmounted photograph (20.7 × 13.3 cm); DKKk.
140. Peter Elfelt, December 1906; C.c. (plate no. 4353); DKKk.
141. Peter Elfelt, November 1908; neg. (plate no. 5623); DKKk.
142. Holger Damgaard, taken for the production January 8, 1926; neg.; DKKk. Photograph taken on the stage of the Royal Theatre. Scenery arranged by Thorolf Pedersen (1926) with only minor changes from his own previous set (see no. 137). In use until 1929.
143. August Birch, taken between October 1867 and 1876; C. de v.; DKKt.
144. Peter Elfelt, November 1909; neg. (plate no. 5999); DKKk.
145. Peter Newland, May 1915; C.c. (plate no. 24450); E. Merrild collection.
146. Harald Paetz, November 24, 1867; C. de v.; DKKt.
147. N. C. Hansen and F. C. L. Weller, taken between 1877 and 1885; C. de v.; DKKt.

148. Unknown photographer, taken for the production March 15, 1914 or earlier (1903?); unmounted photograph (12.9 × 17.9 cm); DKKkt. Scenery originally by C. F. Christensen (1842). Repainted with minor alterations by Valdemar Gyllich (1875) in order to fit the dimensions of the new theatre. New sets painted by Thorolf Pedersen in 1898 (see no. 149) and again in 1903 (seen here) with enlarged dimensions. In use until 1923.
149. Frederik Riise, taken between October 10, 1898 and March 19, 1899; photograph (16.7 × 22.7 cm) mounted on carton (19.2 × 24 cm); DKKt. Photograph taken on the stage of the Royal Theatre. Scenery repainted by Thorolf Pedersen (1898). In use until 1902. This photograph was first published in *Hver 8. Dags Musik og Sang* (March 19, 1899). It represents only the second known picture taken on the stage of the Royal Theatre (the first known picture taken on stage is from *The Valkyrie,* Act IV (final scene) and was published in *Illustreret Tidende,* January 1, 1895, p. 229. The picture here is interesting because it shows the original costumes of the tritons and a naiad holding the veil that covered the lifeless Teresina when she came drifting into the grotto. This veil symbolised her lifeless state and is as such a clear allusion to Giselle's veil in Act II of *Giselle,* seen by Bournonville in Paris in 1841 only six months prior to the premiere of *Napoli.*
150. Sofus Peter Christensen and E. L. & L. J. Morange, c. 1885; C.c.; DKKk.
151. Mads Alstrup (?); c. 1844; laterally reversed hand-coloured daguerreotype (here reproduced as the original); small half-plate (13.1 × 10.5 cm) with sight 9.1 × 6.5 cm in a pink *passepartout* with 4 golden frames; DKKt. Marie Cathrine Werning (von Kohl: 1822–1900) was the daughter of the famous ballerina, the elder Marie Cathrine Werning (d'Abis: 1798–1871). The younger Werning, however, never reached the same heights as her mother, but was engaged as *Figurantinde* (ordinary member of the corps de ballet) from 1842 to 1857 when she left the theatre after marriage to the lawyer Mathias Frederik August von Kohl. The daguerreotype was in all probability taken by Mads Alstrup in 1844. That year the photographer opened a studio in the same pavilion of the Christiansborg Palace that housed the Court Theatre – at that time used as the rehearsal stage of the Royal Ballet. It is thus most likely that Werning had her picture taken during a dress rehearsal at the nearby Court Theatre in May or August 1844. Another fact, which points to Alstrup as the photographer, is the pink *passepartout* and the coloured plate. Alstrup is the only photographer at that time known to have used coloured *passepartouts* (although mostly blue). Moreover, he was highly praised for his *coloured* daguerreotype portraits, shown in an exhibition in *Industriforeningen* (August 1844) and at the Academy of Fine Arts (Autumn 1844). (See Ochsner, *Fotografer i og fra Danmark til og med år 1920,* pp. 109–11). The daguerreotype represents the earliest known Danish ballet photograph and must be one of the earliest *preserved* ballet photographs in the world. Although a series of daguerreotypes (depicting Fanny Cerrito, Marie Guy-Stéphan, Louise Fleury and Henri Desplaces) is known to have been taken by Antoine Claudet in London at the end of June 1842 (see Ivor Guest, *Fanny Cerrito,* p. 45–46,) no other preserved daguerreotypes earlier than the Danish has been traced so far. Two daguerreotypes later than the Danish are known however: (a) daguerreotype by Friedrich Wilhelm Dost (Berlin, 1846), showing a group of five unidentified dancers or acrobats (?: three men and two women) and a violinist, in what appears to be an arranged rehearsal situation; (b) daguerreotype by Carl Ferdinand Stelzner (Hamburg, c. 1849) showing Fanny Elssler in Italian dance costume (*La Tarentule* ?). Both daguerreotypes are reproduced in Fritz Kempe, *Daguerreotypie in Deutschland* (pp. 56, 126), the latter being wrongly identified as Marie Taglioni. The time of exposure for a daguerreotype in the 1840s was about 15–30 seconds, which has apparently caused Werning some trouble in holding her pose. Her left hand (on the reversed daguerreotype appearing as her right) has thus clearly been moved during the time of exposure. The coloured daguerreotype testifies to the original colours of the naiads' costumes, which were made within a scale of two colours: a bluish-silvery corset and a greenish-turquoise tutu with stripes of attached silver spangles. With all the naiads on stage, these costumes added a strong visual effect to C. F. Christensen's magic *grotta d'azzurra* scenery.
152. Harald Paetz, taken between March 1873 and March 1885; C. de v.; DKKt.
153. Theodor Collin, March 29, 1862 (outdoor shot); C. de v.; DKKt.
154. Sofus Peter Christensen and E. L. & L. J. Morange, c. 1885; C.c.; DKKk.
155. Unknown photographer, taken for the production March 15, 1914 or earlier (1903?); unmounted photograph (12.9 × 17.9 cm); DKKkt. Scenery originally by C. F. Christensen (1842). Repainted by Valdemar Gyllich (1875) with a number of changes (a new bridge with only *one* arch and an altarpiece of the Virgin Mary situated between the second and third wing of stage right) in order to fit the dimensions of the new theatre. Repainted by Thorolf Pedersen (1898 & 1903) with only minor alterations from Gyllich's set. In use until 1923.
156. Emil Hohlenberg, c. 1885; C. de v.; DKKt.

This carte-de-visite photograph is the earliest known picture of Hans Beck in the rôle of Gennaro, which he performed with unrivalled mastery for thirty years until his farewell performance on May 29, 1915.

157. Peter Elfelt, January 1905; neg. (plate no. 3605); DKKk.
158. Peter Elfelt, May 1909; neg. (plate no. 5844); DKKk.
Note the supreme mastery with which the two dancers here demonstrate a classic Bournonville pose. The original Bournonville postures (today often strongly moderated if not totally omitted) always consisted of a fascinating interplay of soft and naturally curved lines between the two sexes, as can be seen on this photograph. It was this intricate art of posing which Bournonville later fully developed in ballets like *Psyche* (1850) and *Abdallah* (1855).
159. Peter Elfelt, May 1909; neg. (plate no. 5826); DKKk.
160. Unknown photographer, taken between October 1864 and January 1871; C. de v.; DKKt.
161. Holger Damgaard, taken for the production December 29, 1928; neg.; DKKk. Photograph taken on the stage of the Royal Theatre. Scenery repainted by Thorolf Pedersen (1926) with only minor changes from his previous set (1898). In use until 1929.
162. Georg E. Hansen & Co., taken between June 1870 and 1871; C. de v.; DKKt.
163. Same as no. 162.
Note the photographer's attempt to create a true 'Italian' milieu by adding a flower stand with orange trees.
164. Peter Elfelt, May 27, 1903; neg. (plate no. 3853); DKKk.
Nos. 164 and 165 are enlargements of frames from a film (30 metres) originally shot by Elfelt in May 1903 (Elfelt moving picture neg. no. 59).
165. Peter Elfelt, May 27, 1903; neg. (plate no. 3855); DKKk.
166. Peter Elfelt, May 1909; neg. (plate no. 5853); DKKk.
Nos. 158–159 and 166–167 are showcase photographs taken for a summer tour to Berlin in 1909. The four dancers performed an adapted version of the *Pas de six* and *Tarantella* as an independent group named *De Fire* (The Four).
167. Peter Elfelt, May 1909; neg. (plate no. 5854); DKKk.
168. Peter Elfelt, May 1904; neg. (plate no. 3418); DKKk.
Note the dancer's stays, tied upon her blouse. This type of stays permitted her to change dress rapidly between the *Tarantella* and the Finale. The stays were in use until 1956.
169. Peter Elfelt, May 1907; neg. (plate no. 4724); DKKk.
170. Holger Damgaard, taken for the production December 29, 1928; neg.; DKKk. Photograph taken on the stage of the Royal Theatre. Scenery repainted by Thorolf Pedersen (1928) with only minor changes from his own previous set (1926 – see no. 173). In use until 1929. According to dancer Edel Pedersen this picture shows a group that never appeared in the Finale of the 1928 production. The photograph is most likely an 'extra', taken at the request of the photographer, since both men from the *Pas de six* and girls from the *Bacchanalian Finale* are seen here together in a grouping that never occurs in the actual finale.
171. Peter Elfelt, December 1902; neg. (plate no. 2843); DKKk.
172. Peter Elfelt, April 22, 1905; neg. (plate no. 3723); DKKk.
173. Frederik Riise, taken between October 10, 1898 and April 2, 1899; photograph (16.7 × 22.7 cm) mounted on carton (19.2 × 24 cm); DKKt.
Photograph taken on the stage of the Royal Theatre. Scenery repainted by Thorolf Pedersen (1898). In use until 1902. This photograph (first published in *Hver 8. Dags Musik og Sang*, April 2, 1899) is interesting because it shows the original final grouping with two pairs from *Pas de six* in attitudes at each side of the cart – a grouping which has been abandoned in today's performances.
174. Sofus Peter Christensen and E. L. & L. J. Morange, c. 1880–84; C.c.; DKKt.
175. Theodor Collin, c. 1861–62 (outdoor shot); C. de v.; DKKt.
176. Unknown photographer, taken for the production December 1, 1912; photograph (11.6 × 17 cm) mounted in *Maskinmesterprotokol 20, serie 1* (1912–13); DKKkt.
Scenery originally arranged by C. F. Christensen (1849) with use of older sets. Rearranged by Valdemar Gyllich (1874) from various older sets in order to fit the dimensions of the new theatre. Repainted with only minor alterations by Thorolf Pedersen (1897). In use until 1934. Note (on stage left) the noticeboard on the wall with the daily list of rehearsals, and the two portraits (Vestris and Gardel).
177. Peter Elfelt, November 1909; neg. (plate no. 5993); DKKk.
178. Peter Elfelt, November 1909; neg. (plate no. 5994); DKKk.
179. Peter Elfelt, c. 1912; C.c.; E. Beck collection.
In the original version of *Conservatoriet* there was no old fiddler to accompany the *Pas d'école*. This character was first introduced by Harald Lander in his production on December 3, 1933 (see no. 181). Before this Alexis accompanied the class on his *pochette* (in this photograph, however, shown with a violin) until the arrival of Ernesto, who accompanies Eliza, Victorine and Alexis in their performance of 'A brilliant pas de trois'.

180. Unknown photographer, March 1879; C.c.; DKKt.
Anna Tychsen performed the rôle of Eliza only four times in March 1879.
181. Holger Damgaard, taken for the production December 3, 1933; neg.; DKKk. Photograph taken on the stage of the Royal Theatre. Scenery repainted by Thorolf Pedersen (1897). In use until 1934.
182. Same as no. 181.
183. Peter Elfelt, November 1909; neg. (plate no. 5995); DKKk.
184. Unknown photographer, taken for the production December 1, 1912; photograph (11.6 × 17 cm) mounted in *Maskinmesterprotokol 20, serie 1* (1912–13); DKKkt.
Scenery originally arranged by C. F. Christensen (1849) with use of older sets. Rearranged by Valdemar Gyllich (1874) from various older sets in order to fit the dimensions of the new theatre. Repainted with only minor alterations by Thorolf Pedersen (1897). In use until 1934.
185. Peter Newland, November 1912; C.c. (plate no. 21450); E. Merrild collection.
186. Edvard Møller, taken between September 1898 and September 16, 1899; unmounted photograph (14 × 10.4 cm); E. Freddie collection.
187. Peter Elfelt, November 1909; neg. (plate no. 5996); DKKk.
188. Peter Elfelt, December 9, 1912; neg. (plate no. 6985); DKKk.
189. Theodor Collin, c. 1861–62 (outdoor shot); C. de v.; DKKt.
190. Holger Damgaard, taken for the production December 3, 1933; neg.; DKKk. Photograph taken on the stage of the Royal Theatre. Scenery repainted by Thorolf Pedersen (1897). In use until 1934.
191. Same as no. 190.
192. Same as no. 190.
193. Unknown photographer, taken for the production September 9, 1900; unmounted photograph (11.6 × 16.9 cm); DKKt.
Scenery originally arranged by C. F. Christensen (1851) with use of older sets. Rearranged by Valdemar Gyllich (1875) with use of various older sets in order to fit the dimensions of the new theatre. Repainted with only minor alterations by Thorolf Pedersen in 1900 (seen here). In use until 1926. Note the (faint) silhouette of the cathedral of Notre-Dame in Bruges painted on the back-cloth.
The scenery of *The Kermesse in Brüges* consisted originally of four sets:
Act I: A market place in Brüges.
Act II, first set: Mirewelt's study.
Act II, second set: A magnificent garden at the Castle of Everdingen.
Act III, first set: As Act II, first set.
Act III, second set: Transformation to a large open square on the outskirts of the town.
For the first restaging of the ballet at the new Royal Theatre (January 10, 1875) the second set of Act III was replaced by the scenery of Act I, but with a few alterations such as a stake erected in centre stage and the judge's writing desk (seen on this photograph). After the production on September 9, 1900 the opening scene of Act III (in Mirewelt's study) was omitted and replaced by a procession of the prisoners and their executioners, performed in front of the lowered curtain.
194. Peter Elfelt, March 1910; neg. (plate no. 6175); DKKk.
The *Slovanka* was originally performed in Act III of Bournonville's Hungarian ballet *In the Carpathians* (premiered on March 4, 1857). From this very shortlived ballet Bournonville arranged a divertissement named *The Pitman's Dream* (premiered on November 6, 1859) which included four dances of Act I and the *Slovanka* from Act III. Of this divertissement only the *Slovanka* has survived after it was incorporated as a divertissement in Act I of *The Kermesse in Bruges* at its restaging on November 11, 1865.
195. Sofus Peter Christensen and E. L. & L. J. Morange, 1884; C.c.; DKKt.
196. Peter Elfelt, September 30, 1905; neg. (plate no. 3901); DKKk.
197. Peter Elfelt, September 30, 1905; neg. (plate no. 3900); DKKk.
198. Unknown photographer, taken for the production September 9, 1900; neg.; DKKt.
Scenery originally arranged by C. F. Christensen (1851) with use of older sets. Rearranged by Valdemar Gyllich (1875) with use of various older sets in order to fit the dimensions of the new theatre. Repainted with only minor alterations by Thorolf Pedersen in 1900 (seen here). In use until 1926. This décor was also used with minor alterations in Act II of Friedrich Kuhlau's national fairy play *The Elves' Hill* at its restaging in the new Royal Theatre on December 26, 1883.
199. Peter Elfelt, November 1909; neg. (plate no. 5984); DKKk.
200. Same as no. 198.
201. Same as no. 198.
202. Peter Elfelt, November 1909; neg. (plate no. 5985); DKKk.
203. Peter Elfelt, November 1909; neg. (plate no. 5986); DKKk.
204. Frederik Schmidt and Rasmus Malling, taken between November 1865 and 1867; photograph (26.7 × 19.4 cm) in frame; DKKt.
205. Peter Elfelt, November 1909; neg. (plate no. 5989); DKKk.

206. Unknown photographer, taken for the production September 9, 1900; neg.; DKKkt.
Scenery originally arranged by C. F. Christensen (1851) with use of older sets. Rearranged by Valdemar Gyllich (1875) with use of various older sets in order to fit the dimensions of the new theatre. New scenery arranged by Thorolf Pedersen in 1900 (seen here) with sets taken partially from Act II of Mozart's opera *The Marriage of Figaro* (restaged on December 17, 1899). In use until 1926. This set also served as décor for Marius Petipa's ballet *Les Millions d'Harlequin*, premiered on December 9, 1906 with new choreography devised by Emilie Walbom.
207. Peter Elfelt, November 1909; neg. (plate no. 6005); DKKk.
208. Theodor Collin, c. 1861–62 (outdoor shot); C. de v.; DKKt.
209. Albert Schou, taken between 1891–93; C.c.; DKKt.
210. Sophus Juncker-Jensen, c. 1909; photograph (14.9 × 10.4 cm) mounted on carton; M. Castenskiold collection.
211. Peter Elfelt, November 1909; neg. (plate no. 5992); DKKk.
212. Peter Elfelt, November 1909; neg. (plate no. 6010); DKKk.
213. Unknown photographer, taken for the production May 4, 1929 or earlier (1903?); neg.; DKKkt.
Scenery originally by Troels Lund (1853). Rearranged by Valdemar Gyllich (1880) with use of older sets in order to fit the dimensions of the new theatre. Repainted with only minor alterations by Thorolf Pedersen (1903). In use until May 10, 1929, when the ballet was given its last performance.
214. Peter Elfelt, February 1911; C.c. (plate no. 6575); DKKt.
This photograph is the first in a series of twelve showcase photographs shot by Elfelt in his studio in Østergade 24. The series, of which eleven are reproduced here, is one of the most important photographic sources for this ballet. It illustrates *the mimic art of postures* in the true Bournonville conception of these words – an art of mimic expressions which he in his memoirs named 'the dramatic truth'. It looks as if Elfelt must have been assisted by ballet-master Hans Beck during the shooting of this series. Beck must have given the dancers instructions on how to 'perform' what he considered the most characteristic dramatic episodes in this ballet. Owing to lack of space in the studio the shooting of the series resulted in groupings which in some cases (nos. 232–233) appear more 'compressed' than they must have been on stage. On many of the pictures the roll with back-cloth and carpet is visible, serving as a demarcation line for the dancer, not to be crossed during the shooting. The series also reveals the rather peculiar fact that dancers were occasionally depicted in rôles they never had performed on stage: such is the case of Grethe Ditlevsen, who was never to perform the rôle of Ragnhild.
215. Peter Elfelt, September 30, 1905; neg. (plate no. 3896); DKKk.
216. Peter Elfelt, September 30, 1905; neg. (plate no. 3895); DKKk.
217. Peter Elfelt, February 1911; C.c. (plate no. 6576); DKKt.
218. Peter Elfelt, September 30, 1905; neg. (plate no. 3898); DKKk.
219. Peter Elfelt, February 1911; neg. (plate no. 6574); DKKk.
220. Peter Elfelt, February 1911; neg. (plate no. 6573); DKKt.
221. Peter Elfelt, October 1907; neg. (plate no. 4856); DKKk.
222. Peter Elfelt, February 1911; neg. (plate no. 6572); DKKk.
223. Peter Elfelt, May 1903; neg. (plate no. 2980); DKKk.
224. Unknown photographer, taken for the production March 4, 1929; or earlier (1903?); neg.; DKKkt.
Scenery originally by C. F. Christensen (1853). Rearranged by Valdemar Gyllich (1880) with use of older sets in order to fit the dimensions of the new theatre. Repainted with only minor alterations by Thorolf Pedersen (1903). In use until May 10, 1929, when the ballet was given its last performance.
225. Emil Hohlenberg, 1881; C.c.; DKKk.
226. Peter Elfelt, May 1903; C.c. (plate no. 2970); M. Castenskiold collection.
227. Theodor Collin, c. 1861–62 (outdoor shot); C. de v.; DKKt.
228. N. C. Hansen and Clemens Weller (?), taken between January 1880 and October 1884; unmounted photograph (13.8 × 9.4 cm); DKKk.
This photograph is included in a collection of negatives (glass plates) that appears to have been taken by Hansen and Weller and is preserved in the Theatre Museum. Note the chalk lines around the dancers' feet, drawn by the photographer in order to mark their fixed position during the exposure time.
229. Peter Elfelt, May 1903; neg. (plate no. 2983); DKKk.
230. Peter Elfelt, February 1911; neg. (plate no. 6585); DKKt.
231. Holger Damgaard, taken for the production May 4, 1929; unmounted photograph (15.2 × 22.7 cm); DKKkt.
Photograph taken on the stage of the Royal Theatre. Scenery repainted by Thorolf Pedersen (1903). In use until May 10, 1929.
232. Peter Elfelt, February 1911; neg. (plate no. 6577); DKKk.
233. Peter Elfelt, February 1911; neg. (plate no. 6578); DKKk.
234. Peter Elfelt, February 1911; neg. (plate no. 6579); DKKk.

235. Jens August Schultz, taken between February and March 1884; C.c.; DKKk.
236. Emil Hohlenberg, 1881; C.c.; DKKk.
237. Peter Elfelt, February 1911; neg. (plate no. 6581); DKKk.
238. Peter Elfelt, September 30, 1905; neg. (plate no. 3899); DKKk.
239. Sofus Peter Christensen and E. L. & L. J. Morange, taken between 1891 and 1895; C.c.; DKKt.
240. Peter Elfelt, February 1911; neg. (plate no. 6583); DKKk.
241. Unknown photographer, taken for the production May 4, 1929 or earlier (1903?); neg.; DKKkt.
Scenery originally by Troels Lund (1853). Rearranged by Valdemar Gyllich (1880) with use of older sets in order to fit the dimensions of the new theatre. Repainted with only minor alterations by Thorolf Pedersen (1903). In use until May 10, 1929 when the ballet was given its last performance.
242. Peter Elfelt, May 1903; neg. (plate no. 2981); DKKk.
243. Peter Elfelt, May 1903; neg. (plate no. 2982); DKKk.
244. Holger Damgaard, taken for the production May 4, 1929; neg.; DKKk.
Photograph taken on the stage of the Royal Theatre. Scenery repainted by Thorolf Pedersen (1903). In use until May 10, 1929.
245. Peter Newland, May 1920; unmounted photograph (15.8 × 11.7 cm); E. Merrild collection.
Showcase photograph taken for a summer tour in Denmark arranged and directed by Karl Merrild, 1920. The idea for this dance may stem from a popular Norwegian game which became widespread at the beginning of the nineteenth century. The origin of this game, however, is much older, deriving from the institution of the barbers' guild in Bergen in 1597. To become a member of the guild all candidates had to undergo a rather coarse jest, being smeared with a foam of all kinds of filthiness before the shaving ceremony.
246. Peter Elfelt, May 1903; neg. (plate no. 2984); DKKk.
247. Same as no. 244.
248. Same as no. 244.
249. Peter Elfelt, March 1904; neg. (plate no. 3271); DKKk.
250. Unknown photographer, taken for the performance on May 10, 1908; neg.; DKKkt.
Scenery originally by C. F. Christensen (1854). New scenery by Fritz Ahlgrensson (1874) with partial use of older sets and props in order to fit the dimensions of the new theatre. New set painted by Valdemar Gyllich for the production on April 29, 1894 (seen here). In use until 1919.
251. Theodor Collin, c. 1861/62 (outdoor shot); C. de v.; DKKt.
252. Sophus Juncker-Jensen, 1907; C.c.; M. Castenskiold collection.
253. Unknown photographer, taken for the production September 24, 1922; photograph (12 × 17 cm) mounted in *Maskinmesterprotokol, Mappe 39 nr. 5*; DKKkt.
Scenery originally by C. F. Christensen (1854). New scenery by Fritz Ahlgrensson (1874) with partial use of older sets and props in order to fit the dimensions of the new theatre. New set by Valdemar Gyllich (1894). Repainted with only minor alterations from Gyllich's set by Thorolf Pedersen for the production on September 24, 1922 (seen here). In use until 1931.
254. William Augustinus, 1894; C.c. (plate no. 327: Elfelt plate no. 6790); DKKk.
This photograph is the first in a series of six taken by Augustinus in the autumn of 1894. Five pictures from this series have been reproduced here (nos. 254, 261, 263, 265, 269). Augustinus' original negatives (glass plates) were later bought by Peter Elfelt and registered in his archive in August 1911, when they were given new plate numbers. Since some of the original glass negatives have been damaged three of the photographs have here been reproduced from cabinet cards.
255. Harald Paetz, c. 1870; C. de v.; DKKt.
256. Valdemar Riis Knudsen, November 1913; photograph mounted on carton (16.9 × 23 cm); E. Freddie collection.
Photograph taken on the stage of Århus Teater for the production on November 9, 1913 of a dramatisation of Bournonville's ballet. This five act fairy play, in which Hilda appears as a mimic part with two larger solos, was written by Edgar Collin, Alfred Ipsen and Vilhelm Østergaard and premiered at the Folketeatret (Copenhagen) on December 26, 1892. A score based on Hartmann's and Gade's original music was arranged by Nicolai Hansen, who added a number of choruses of his own. The play, the only dramatisation ever of a Bournonville ballet, achieved great success and was staged in a number of other theatres in Denmark (Casino Theatre, Copenhagen, on March 15, 1911, and Odense Friluftsteater, Odense, on June 13, 1916 – see no. 267). The scenery for the Århus production (shown here) was by Emil Poulsen. In use until 1914.
257. Holger Damgaard, taken for the production September 1, 1929; neg.; DKKk.
Photograph taken on the stage of the Royal Theatre. Scenery repainted with only minor alterations by Thorolf Pedersen (1922). In use until 1931.
258. Harry Paetz, c. 1895; C.c.; DKKk.
Photograph of painting (oil on canvas) by unknown artist. Location unknown.
259. Unknown photographer, taken for the production September 24, 1922; photo-

graph (12 × 17 cm) mounted in *Maskinmesterprotokol, Mappe 39 nr. 5*; DKKkt. Scenery originally by Troels Lund (1854). New scenery by Fritz Ahlgrensson (1874) in order to fit the dimensions of the new theatre. New set painted by Valdemar Gyllich for the production on April 29, 1894 (seen here). In use until 1944. In Svend Kragh-Jacobsen's and Torben Krogh's *Den Kongelige Danske Ballet* (see Bibliography) Ahlgrensson's sketch for the 1874 décor of Act II is reproduced between pp. 272 and 273. It is claimed, mistakenly that this set was in continuous use until 1944. It was, however, already replaced in 1894 by Gyllich's set, which from then on was the only scenery to be kept unchanged until October 9, 1944. In 1894 the critic of *Nationaltidende* (April 30) remembered Ahlgrensson's 1874 set as more 'funny' and 'imaginative' with its numerous transparent effects in comparison with Gyllich's new set, which, however, impressed the critic by its amazing use of electrical lights and flash lamps during the troll dance.

260. N. C. Hansen and Clemens Weller?, taken between 1884 and 1888; unmounted photograph (13.8 × 9.4 cm); DKKk.
A negative (glass plate) of this photograph, which appears to have been taken by Hansen and Weller, is preserved in the Theatre Museum (see also note for no. 228).

261. William Augustinus, 1894; C.c. (plate no. 329: Elfelt plate no. 6792); DKKk.
262. Carl Schreiber, c. December 1903; C.c.; DKKt.
263. William Augustinus, 1894; neg. (plate no. 330: Elfelt plate no. 6793); DKKk.
264. August Birch, taken between October 1867 and January 1876; C. de v.; DKKt.
265. William Augustinus, 1894; C.c. (plate no. 331: Elfelt plate no. 6794); DKKk.
266. Harald Paetz, c. 1867; C. de v.; DKKt.
267. Holger A. Nielsen, taken June, 1916; P.c.; DKKt.
Photograph taken at Odense open air theatre for a production of the dramatisation of Bournonville's ballet on June 13, 1916 (see also note for no. 256). The photograph was first published in *Teatret* 1915–16 (p. 136) but was later also published as a postcard. It shows Elna Jørgen-Jensen in the mimic part as Hilda, a rôle she performed only in this dramatisation of Bournonville's ballet, never in the actual ballet.

268. Unknown photographer, taken for the production September 24, 1922; photograph (12 × 17 cm) mounted in *Maskinmesterprotokol, Mappe 39 nr. 5*; DKKkt. Scenery originally by C. F. Christensen (1854). New scenery by Fritz Ahlgrensson (1874) with partial use of older sets and props in order to fit the dimensions of the new theatre. New set (representing a cornfield with the manor house in the distance and, to the right, a hillside in front of which the harvested corn was placed in stooks) painted by Valdemar Gyllich for the production on April 29, 1894.
In the original production (1854) Act III consisted of only two sets:
1. Scenes 1–3 & 5–6 and final score: The outskirts of a forest.
2. Scene 4: Frøken Birthe's chamber in the manor house (see no. 271).
For the production on September 24, 1922, Thorolf Pedersen extended the first set of Act III by painting two new sceneries: one for scenes 1–3 (seen here) and another for scenes 5–6 and final score (see no. 276). Both of these were in use until 1931. Against this, the décor of scene 4 (Birthe's chamber) was kept unchanged from the previous 1894 production (see no. 271).

269. William Augustinus, 1894; neg. (plate no. 332: Elfelt plate no. 6795); DKKk.
270. Emil Hohlenberg, taken between 1881 and 1899; C. de v.; DKKt.
271. Unknown photographer, taken for the performance on May 10, 1908; unmounted photograph (12.7 × 17.9 cm); DKKkt.
Scenery originally by Troels Lund (1854). New set arranged by Fritz Ahlgrensson (1874) with use of older décors in order to fit the dimensions of the new theatre. Repainted with only minor alterations by Valdemar Gyllich in 1894 (seen here). In use until 1931.

272. Harald Paetz, c. 1870; C. de v.; DKKt.
273. Theodor Collin, c. 1861–62 (outdoor shot); C. de v.; DKKt.
Note the photographer's attempt to make the dancer appear to have a slender waist by touching up her figure – an attempt rarely seen in this early period of photography.

274. Harald Paetz, c. 1870; C. de v.; DKKt.
275. Sophus Juncker-Jensen, 1907; C.c.; M. Castenskiold collection.
276. Unknown photographer, taken for the production September 24, 1922; photograph (12 × 17 cm) mounted in *Maskinmesterprotokol Mappe 39 nr. 5*; DKKkt. New scenery painted by Thorolf Pedersen for the production on September 24, 1922 (see note for no. 268). In use until 1931.

277. Harry Paetz, c. 1896; C.c.; DKKt.
278. Harald Paetz, 1868; C. de v.; DKKk.
279. Carl Schreiber, c. December 1903; C.c.; DKKt.
Richard Jensen made his début in the *Pas de sept* of *A Folk Tale*, which was the occasion for the taking of this picture. Note his fine placement of the upper body and the characteristic position of the rounded hands with the thumb slightly touching the forefinger – a typical Bournonville feature neglected all too often in today's performances.

280. Peter Newland, October 14, 1922; unmounted photograph (15.8 × 11.7 cm); E. Merrild collection.
Note the significant difference of the costumes in this and the previous photograph, covering a period of only twenty years!

281. Unknown photographer, taken for the production September 3, 1907; photograph (11.4 × 16.9 cm) mounted in *Maskinmesterprotokol 15, serie 1* (1907–8); DKKkt.
Scenery originally arranged by C. F. Christensen (1854) New scenery arranged from various older sets by Valdemar Gyllich (1875) in order to fit the dimensions of the new theatre. For the performance on January 9, 1897, Thorolf Pedersen adapted an older set (seen here), previously used in Act II of Shakespeare's *The Merchant of Venice* (restaged on May 10, 1896). This set was in use until 1915.

282. Harald Paetz, taken between March 1871 and April 1872; C. de v.; DKKt. Note the topknot on the Señorita's dress, which she later tosses down to the serenading Señor as a sign that his homage has been acknowledged.

283. N. C. Hansen and F. C. L. Weller, taken between 1877 and May 1879; C. de v.; DKKt.
Note the peculiar way in which the dancer is portrayed on this rare photograph – taken deliberately from behind in order to give a lifelike representation of the reversed mirror dance.

284. Same as no. 282.
285. Peter Elfelt, October 1907; neg. (plate no. 4895); DKKk.
This photograph is part of a series of nine taken by Elfelt in 1907 when Ellen Price de Plane first performed the part of the Señorita. From this series, which covers situations from both of the ballet's two sections, three pictures are selected and reproduced here (nos. 285, 286, 291).

286. Peter Elfelt, October 1907; neg. (plate no. 4898); DKKk.
287. Harald Paetz, 1868; C. de v.; DKKt.
This photograph is part of a series of twelve portraits of the leading female artists of the Royal Theatre, photographed between 1868 and 1870 and sold from November 4, 1870, as a collection named *Bouquet des dames*. The copy in the Theatre Museum of Anna Scholl's portrait in *La Ventana* is dated with the inscription 'photographeert 1868'.

288. Unknown photographer, taken for the production September 3, 1907; photograph (11.4 × 16.9 cm) mounted in *Maskinmesterprotokol 15, serie 1* (1907–8); DKKkt.
Scenery originally painted by C. F. Christensen (1856). New scenery arranged by Valdemar Gyllich (1875) with use of various older sets and props in order to fit the dimensions of the new theatre. Rearranged with only minor alterations by Thorolf Pedersen in 1897 and again in 1907 (seen here). In use until 1915.

289. N. C. Hansen and F. C. L. Weller, November 1882; C. de v.; DKKt.
290. Peter Elfelt, March 1908; neg. (plate in oblong no. 5206); DKKk.
One of the rare Elfelt photographs taken in oblong with a dancer holding an attitude (here *attitude bras opposé*). The *Pas de trois* in *La Ventana*, one of Bournonville's technically most demanding dances, was occasionally performed by three ladies in the 1890s and at the beginning of this century (last time on October 4, 1907) in spite of the original casting being for a man and two women.

291. Peter Elfelt, October 1907; neg. (plate no. 4895); DKKk.
292. E. Lange, taken between October 1862 and 1863; C. de v.; DKKt.
293. Georg Rosenkilde, 1864; C. de v.; DKKt.
294. Theodor Collin, c. 1861–62 (outdoor shot); C. de v.; DKKt.
295. Peter Elfelt, c. May 1906; neg. (plate no. 4143); DKKk.
296. Peter Elfelt, c. May 1906; neg. (plate no. 4142); DKKk.
297. Harald Paetz, c. December 1867; C. de v.; DKKt.
298. Christian Reinau, October 1903; C.c.; DKKt.
299. Sophus Juncker-Jensen, taken between December 28, 1919 and February 23, 1920; unmounted photograph (10.7 × 22.3 cm); E. Merrild collection.
Photograph taken on the stage of the Royal Theatre, showing the second cast in Gustav Uhlendorff's production of the entire ballet (premiered on December 26, 1919). Scenery originally by C. F. Christensen (1858). New scenery by Valdemar Gyllich (1877) with partial use of older sets in order to fit the dimensions of the new theatre (in use until September 16, 1906). New scenery painted by Thorolf Pedersen for the production of the entire ballet on December 29, 1919 (seen here). In use until 1922.

300. Emil Rye, taken between 1872 and 1877; C. de v.; DKKt.
301. Peter Newland, November 1929; C.c.; E. Merrild collection.
302. Unknown photographer, taken for the production of Section 2 on February 19, 1910; photograph (11.4 × 16.9 cm) mounted in *Scenebilledalbum (grå)*, p. 167; DKKkt.
Scenery originally by Troels Lund (1858). New scenery by Valdemar Gyllich

(1877) with partial use of older sets in order to fit the dimensions of the new theatre. Rearranged by Gyllich for the production of Section 2 on February 25, 1894 with partial use of older sets from Ludvig Holberg's five-act Spanish comedy *Don Ranudo de Colibrados* (restaged at the new theatre on February 21, 1894). New scenery painted by Thorolf Pedersen for the production of Section 2 on February 19, 1910 (seen here). In use until 1922.

303. Sophus Juncker-Jensen, 1910; C.c.; DKKk.

304. Georg Lindström, October 1902; C.c.; Mary Clarke collection.
Danish born Adeline Genée appeared at Copenhagen's Royal Theatre in a series of guest performances from October 23 to November 5, 1902. She performed in *Coppélia*, in an unspecified pas de deux (with Gustav Uhlendorff), and as Rosa in *The Flower Festival in Genzano*. The critic of *Politiken* (October 24, 1902) found her dancing less expressive than that of the dancers of the Royal Theatre, particularly in the *Saltarello* which closed the divertissement: 'The real sphere of this young Anglo-Danish dancer is evidently the purely artistic dance ... there is something mechanical about her dancing, which detracts from the pleasure of renewed acquaintance. One misses variety, warmth, character ... However, the audience was dazzled by the phenomenon, and rejoiced in it. The dancer's slim and pretty figure, reminiscent of one of Hans Christian Andersen's self-important little fairy tale princesses, is so different from the tender, arch and chubby ladies of our own ballet that it pleases by the mere fact of being unusual.'

305. Peter Elfelt, c. February 1906; neg. (plate no. 4051); DKKk.
306. Peter Elfelt, c. February 1906; neg. (plate no. 4052); DKKk.
307. Holger Damgaard, taken for the production on October 15, 1929; neg.; DKKk.
New scenery painted by Thorolf Pedersen for the production of the entire ballet on October 15, 1929 with partial use of his previous set for Section 2 from 1910 (see no. 302). For the 1929 production the scenery was reduced to only one set, namely a combination of the wooded area near Arricia and the main street in Genzano.

308. Peter Elfelt, March 1904; neg. (plate no. 3270); DKKk.
309. Peter Newland, May 1919; unmounted photograph (17 × 22.8 cm); E. Merrild collection.
Showcase photograph taken for a Denmark summer tour arranged and headed by Karl Merrild, 1919. The photograph, probably taken backstage in the Royal Theatre, has a décor arranged for this particular occasion.

310. Unknown photographer, taken between October 9, 1865 and February 21, 1866; photograph (13.8 × 15.7 cm) in frame; DKKt.
This photograph, which bears no photographer's signature, appears to be an outdoor shot. It dates from the second staging of the ballet (October 10, 1865) when Waldemar Price performed the rôle of Christoffer.

311. Theodor Collin, c. 1861–62 (outdoor shot); C. de v.; DKKt.
312. Unknown photographer, taken between October 9, 1865 and February 21, 1866; C. de v.; DKKt.
This photograph is mounted on a pre-printed carte-de-visite carton with a standard ornamentation around the names *Niépce – Talbot – Daguerre* on the back. It appears to have been taken by the same photographer as no. 310 and shot in an outdoor location.

313. Harald Paetz, taken between March 27, 1877 and May 13, 1878; C. de v.; DKKt.
This picture represents one of the rare photographs by Harald Paetz, in which he attempts to create an actual stage illusion by using an appropriate back-cloth and props.

314. Same as no. 313.
315. Unknown photographer, taken for the production January 1, 1908; photograph (11.6 × 17 cm) mounted in album signed 'Ulrik Valentiner 1936'; DKKt.
Scenery originally by Troels Lund (1860). New scenery arranged by Valdemar Gyllich (1876) with partial use of older sets (including Lund's original back-cloth) in order to fit the dimensions of the new theatre (seen here). In use until May 7, 1925. On September 1, 1925 new scenery was painted by Thorolf Pedersen. This represented an open outdoor square with, to the left, Rosita's veranda and, in the background, the Danish frigate. This outdoor scenery was in use until October 28, 1929.

316. Georg Rosenkilde, 1864; C. de v.; DKKk.
Photograph with painted back-cloth. Juliette Price is actually sitting on an ordinary chair (hidden by her dress) and not on the (painted) basket armchair, which was meant to create the illusion of Rosita resting in the hammock.

317. Harald Paetz, taken between 1868 and 1872; C. de v.; DKKt.
318. Peter Elfelt, August 1908; neg. (plate no. 5515); DKKk.
319. Peter Elfelt, February 1908; neg. (plate no. 5036); DKKk.
320. Peter Elfelt, February 1908; neg. (plate no. 5038); DKKk.
321. Holger Damgaard (?), taken for the production on December 26, 1915;

unmounted photograph (23.8 × 17.9 cm); DKKt. Photograph taken in the ballet foyer of the Royal Theatre.

322. Peter Elfelt, August 1908; neg. (plate no. 5507); DKKk.
323. Harald Paetz, 1868; C. de v.; DKKt.
324. Peter Elfelt, August 1908; neg. (plate no. 5502); DKKk.
325. Peter Elfelt, August 1908; neg. (plate no. 5503); DKKk.
326. Peter Elfelt, August 1908; neg. (plate no. 5504); DKKk.
327. Harald Paetz, 1868; C. de v.; DKKt.
328. Sophus Juncker-Jensen, taken between 1908 and 1911; photograph (15.1 × 7.7 cm) mounted on carton; M. Castenskiold collection.
329. Holger Damgaard, taken for the production on December 26, 1915; neg.; DKKk.
330. Unknown photographer, taken for the production September 1, 1925; neg.; DKKkt.
Scenery originally by C. F. Christensen (1860). Repainted with only few alterations by Valdemar Gyllich (1876) in order to fit the dimensions of the new theatre. Remounted by Thorolf Pedersen for the production on September 1, 1925 (seen here). For the production on August 31, 1935, the sun tent was omitted to allow a better view for the audience in the upper balconies of the theatre. For the same production the flags were omitted. Otherwise the scenery was kept unchanged up to the last performance of the ballet given so far (November 29, 1979).

331. Harald Paetz, taken between 1868 and 1872; C. de v.; DKKt.
332. George Rosenkilde, 1864; C. de v.; DKKt.
333. Olaf Gjörup & Co.; c. 1899/1900; C. de v.; DKKt.
334. Peter Newland, May 1920; unmounted photograph (15.8 × 11.7 cm); E. Merrild collection.
Showcase photograph taken for a Denmark summer tour arranged and directed by Karl Merrild, 1920.

335. Peter Elfelt, August 1908; neg. (plate no. 5509); DKKt.
336. Peter Elfelt, November 1908; neg. (plate no. 5615); DKKk.
337. Peter Elfelt, August 1908; neg. (plate no. 5506); DKKk.
338. Same as no. 334.
339. Peter Elfelt, February 1908; neg. (plate no. 5059); DKKk.
340. Peter Elfelt, January 1908; neg. (plate no. 4979); DKKk.
341. Harald Paetz, 1868; C. de v.; DKKt.
This photograph represents one of the earliest ballet photographs in which the photographer has deliberately created a frame of 'fog' by letting the picture fade out from dark into a light oval frame.

342. Peter Elfelt, February 1908; neg. (plate no. 5041); DKKk.
343. Peter Elfelt, February 1908; neg. (plate no. 5640); DKKk.
344. Peter Elfelt, November 1908; neg. (plate no. 5612); DKKk.
345. Same as no. 334.
346. Peter Elfelt, February 1908; neg. (plate no. 5043); DKKk.
347. Unknown photographer, taken for the production August 13, 1905; photograph (12.2 × 17.2 cm) mounted in *Scenebilledalbum (grøn)*, p. 25; DKKt.
Scenery originally arranged by C. F. Christensen (1861) with partial use of older sets. New scenery arranged by Valdemar Gyllich (1876) from older sets in order to fit the dimensions of the new theatre. Completely repainted by Gyllich for the production on December 30, 1894 (seen here). In use until 1906.

348. Peter Elfelt, September 20, 1905; neg. (plate no. 3884); DKKk.
The colourful brilliance of the opening rainbow scene was further accentuated by Heimdal's shining golden Gjallar-Horn.

349. E. Lange, c. 1861; C. de v.; DKKt.
350. William Augustinus, 1895; C.c.; DKKk.
351. Georg Rosenkilde, c. 1871; C.c.; DKKt.
Note the (sky-blue) cloak and the golden arm ring, which indicate Odin's supreme status among the gods.

352. Peter Most, taken between January 1873 and January 1879; C.c.; DKKk.
353. Georg Rosenkilde, c. 1871; C. de v.; DKKt.
354. Unknown photographer, taken for the production August 31, 1905; photograph (12.2 × 17.2 cm) mounted in *Scenebilledalbum (grøn)*, p. 26; DKKt.
Scenery originally arranged by C. F. Christensen (1861) with partial use of older sets. New scenery arranged by Valdemar Gyllich (1876) from older sets in order to fit the dimensions of the new theatre. Rearranged with only minor alterations by Gyllich for the production on December 30, 1894 (seen here). In use until 1906. Note, on centre stage, the upright menhir with runic inscriptions serving as a burial monument to the fallen warrior Rerek (Harald Hildetand's son and the father of Helge).

355. Harald Paetz, c. 1870; C. de v.; DKKt.
356. Harald Paetz, c. 1870; C. de v.; DKKk.
357. Sofus Peter Christensen and E. L. & L. J. Morange, 1894; photograph (39.2 × 28 cm) in frame; E. Beck collection.
358. Theodor Collin, c. 1861–62 (outdoor shot); C. de v.; DKKt.

359. Harald Paetz, c. 1870; C. de v.; DKKt.
360. Peter Elfelt, taken between August 1905 and May 1906; neg. (plate no. 4212); DKKk.
361. Unknown photographer, taken for the production August 31, 1905; photograph (12.2 × 17.2 cm) mounted in *Scenebilledalbum (grøn)*, p. 26; DKKkt. Scenery originally painted by C. F. Christensen (1861). Rearranged by Valdemar Gyllich (1876) from older sets in order to fit the dimensions of the new theatre. Completely repainted by Gyllich for the production on December 30, 1894 (seen here). In use until 1906.
362. Sofus Peter Christensen and E. L. & L. J. Morange, 1894; C.c.; E. Beck collection.
363. Same as no. 362.
364. Holger Damgaard, taken for the production on December 26, 1919; neg.; DKKk.
    Photograph taken in the dance studio of the Royal Theatre.
365. Emil Hohlenberg, taken between December 1894 and June 1896; C.c.; DKKt.
366. Unknown photographer, taken for the production August 31, 1905; photograph (11.4 × 17.1 cm) mounted in album signed 'Ulrik Valentiner 1936'; DKKkt.
    Scenery originally arranged by C. F. Christensen (1861) with partial use of older sets. New scenery arranged by Valdemar Gyllich (1876) from older sets in order to fit the dimensions of the new theatre. Rearranged by Gyllich for the production on December 30, 1894 (seen here) with only minor alterations from his own previous set. In use until 1906. Note the Greek temple, which was painted as an exact replica of the ancient *Segesta* temple on Sicily, erected at the end of the fifth century BC.
367. Sophus Juncker-Jensen, December 1919; photograph (12.4 × 26.5 cm) mounted on carton; DKKkt.
    Photograph taken on the stage of the Royal Theatre. Scenery arranged by Valdemar Gyllich (1876) from older sets in order to fit the dimensions of the new theatre. Rearranged by Gyllich for the production on December 30, 1894 with only minor alterations from his own previous set. Remounted by Thorolf Pedersen for the production on December 26, 1919 (seen here) with only a few alterations. In use until September 29, 1921, when the entire ballet was given its last performance.
368. Peter Newland, December 1919; C.c.; E. Merrild collection.
369. Peter Elfelt, taken between August 1905 and May 1906; neg. (plate no. 3867); DKKk.
    The four leading Greek *danseuses* were dressed in light-blue silk costumes, while the other eight Greek dancers wore white silk dresses (see no. 370).
370. Christian Reinau, taken between August 1905 and May 1906; C.c.; M. Castenskiold collection.
371. E. Lange, c. 1861; C. de v.; DKKt.
372. William Augustinus, 1895; C.c.; DKKk.
373. Harald Paetz, c. 1870; C. de v.; DKKt.
374. Emil Hohlenberg, taken between December 1894 and June 1896; C.c. (bearing only the dealer's name 'Schnitger'); DKKt.
375. Same as no. 374.
376. Harald Paetz, c. 1870; C. de v.; DKKt.
377. Peter Elfelt, June 1906; neg. (plate no. 4215); DKKk.
378. Peter Most, taken between May 14 and June 1, 1883; C.c.; DKKt.
    Note the foot in the lower left corner, which, according to a handwritten note on the original photograph, is that of Waldemar Price. Apparently the photographer has here attempted to make a large group picture, but must have somehow failed. The reason could have been the lens used here or the limited space of the studio located in Kjøbmagergade 18.
379. Georg Rosenkilde, 1864; C. de v.; DKKt.
380. Holger Damgaard, taken for the production on December 26, 1919; neg.; DKKk.
    Photograph taken on the stage of the Royal Theatre. Scenery same as in no. 367 (see note).
381. Unknown photographer, taken for the production August 31, 1905; photograph (12.2 × 17.2 cm) mounted in *Scenebilledalbum (grøn)*, p. 27; DKKkt. Scenery originally arranged by C. F. Christensen (1861) with partial use of older sets. New scenery arranged by Valdemar Gyllich (1876) from older sets in order to fit the dimensions of the new theatre. Completely repainted by Gyllich for the production on December 30, 1894 (seen here). In use until 1906.
382. Theodor Collin (?), c. 1861 (outdoor shot ?); C. de v.; DKKt.
383. Emil Hohlenberg, taken between December 1894 and February 21, 1895; C.c.; DKKk.
384. Unknown photographer, taken for the production August 31, 1905; photograph (12.2 × 17.2 cm) mounted in *Scenebilledalbum (grøn)*, p. 28; DKKkt. Scenery originally arranged by C. F. Christensen (1861) with partial use of older sets. New scenery arranged by Valdemar Gyllich (1876) from older sets

in order to fit the dimensions of the new theatre. Completely repainted by Gyllich for the production on December 30, 1894. Remounted by Thorolf Pedersen for the production on August 31, 1905 (seen here) with only minor alterations from Gyllich's previous set. In use until 1906.
385. Harald Paetz, 1867; C. de v.; DKKt.
386. Harald Paetz, c. 1869; C. de v.; DKKk.
387. Unknown photographer, taken for the production August 31, 1905; photograph (12.2 × 17.2 cm) mounted in *Scenebilledalbum (grøn)*, p. 28; DKKkt. Scenery originally arranged by C. F. Christensen (1861) with partial use of older sets. New scenery arranged by Valdemar Gyllich (1876) from older sets in order to fit the dimensions of the new theatre. Completely repainted by Gyllich for the production on December 30, 1894 (seen here). In use until 1906.
388. Unknown photographer, taken for the production August 31, 1905; photograph (12.2 × 17.2 cm) mounted in *Scenebilledalbum (grøn)*, p. 29; DKKkt. Scenery originally painted by C. F. Christensen (1861). New scenery arranged by Valdemar Gyllich (1876) with partial use of older sets in order to fit the dimensions of the new theatre. Completely new scenery by Gyllich for the production on December 30, 1894 (seen here). In use until 1921. Note the two black ravens, Hugin and Munin, sitting on each side of Odin's High-Seat. They served as Odin's personal messengers and informants, reporting directly to him about the incidents of the nine worlds seen on their flights.
389. Georg Lindström, 1905; photograph (15.3 × 23.3 cm) published in *Teatret*, 1905, *18. hefte* (p. 144); DKKk.
    Photograph taken on the stage of the Royal Theatre on August 31, 1905 at the centennial performance of Bournonville's birthday. Scenery same as in no. 388 (see note).
390. Unknown photographer, taken for the production December 3, 1905; photograph (11.1 × 17 cm) mounted in *Maskinmesterprotokol 13, serie 9* (1905–6); DKKk.
    Scenery originally by C. F. Christensen (1866) with partial use of Troels Lund's décor for the fourth tableau in Bournonville's 1845 ballet *Raphael* (premiered on May 30, 1845). New scenery arranged by Valdemar Gyllich (1875) from older sets in order to fit the dimensions of the new theatre. Remounted by Gyllich for the production on February 23, 1896 (seen here) with only minor alterations from his own previous set. In use until November 21, 1911, when the ballet was given its last performance. Note the seated lay figure (at stage left), which served as the painter Alfred's dummy. In scene four of the ballet's first tableau, the old *scrivano* Paoluccio makes a big fool of himself by flirting with this silent figure, mistakenly believing it to be a living model.
391. Peter Elfelt, February 22, 1906; neg. (plate no. 4048); DKKk.
392. Peter Elfelt, May 1907; neg. (plate no. 4657); DKKk.
393. Peter Elfelt, May 1907; neg. (plate no. 4658); DKKk.
394. Peter Elfelt, May 1907; neg. (plate no. 4659); DKKk.
395. Peter Elfelt, May 1907; neg. (plate no. 4660); DKKk.
396. Peter Elfelt, (?), c. December 1905; P.s.; DKKk.
    Photograph taken in the dance studio of the Royal Theatre. Published as a postcard.
397. Unknown photographer, taken for the production December 3, 1905; photograph (11.1 × 17 cm) mounted in *Maskinmesterprotokol 13, serie 1* (1905–6); DKKk.
    Scenery originally painted by C. F. Christensen (1866) Rearranged by Valdemar Gyllich (1875) with partial use of older sets from Act III of Meyerbeer's opera *Robert le Diable* (the cloister scene) in order to fit the dimensions of the new theatre. Remounted by Gyllich for the production on February 23, 1896 (seen here) with only a few alterations from his own previous set. In use until November 21, 1911, when the ballet was given its last performance. Note the Roman bridge, Ponte Milvio, painted on the back-cloth with a passing train bringing the Danish artist Alfred back to his native land in the ballet's final scene.
398. Harald Paetz, 1867; C. de v.; DKKt.
399. Peter Elfelt, February 22, 1906; neg. (plate no. 4049); DKKk.
    The *Pas de deux* and *Saltarello* were reconstructed in November 1981 by Knud Arne Jürgensen from choreographic notations by Bournonville, now preserved in the Theatre Museum. The reconstruction was first performed at the Theatre Museum on November 22, 1981.
400. Leopold Hartmann, taken between October 1875 and November 1879; C.c.; DKKk.
401. Harald Paetz, c. 1870; C. de v.; DKKt.
402. Peter Elfelt, November 1908; neg. (plate no. 5604); DKKk.
403. Peter Elfelt (?), c. December 1905; P.s.; DKKk.
    Photograph taken in the dance studio of the Royal Theatre. Published as a postcard.
404. Georg Lindström, December 1905; photograph (14.5 × 22 cm) published in *Teatret*, December 19, 1905, 5. *Hefte, V. Aargang*, (p. 52); DKKk.

Photograph taken on the stage of the Royal Theatre. Scenery same as on no. 397 (seen note).

405. Harald Paetz, c. 1870; C. de v.; DKKt.
406. Thor Larsen, April 1919; unmounted photograph (16.7 × 23.9 cm); DKKkt. This is the first in a series of three press photographs taken in the dance studio of the Royal Theatre for a performance of Act I, given at the Casino Theatre (Copenhagen) on April 4, 1919 to celebrate the forthcoming reunification of southern Jutland with the Kingdom of Denmark (see also note for no. 454).
407. Thor Larsen, April 1919; unmounted photograph (15.4 × 22.2 cm); DKKkt. See also note for no. 406.
408. Georg Lindström, 1901; C.c.; E. Beck collection.
409. Thor Larsen, April 1919; unmounted photograph (17.1 × 20.3 cm); DKKkt. See also note for no. 406
410. Harald Paetz, c. 1870; C. de v.; DKKt.
411. Peter Elfelt, November 1904; P.s. (plate no. 3541); DKKk. Photograph taken in the dance studio of the Royal Theatre. Published as a postcard.
412. Georg Lindström, 1901; C.c.; E. Beck collection.
413. Harald Paetz, c. 1870; C. de v.; DKKt.
414. Harald Paetz, c. 1870; C. de v.; DKKt.
415. Georg Lindström, 1901; C.c. (14.9 × 8 cm); E. Beck collection.
416. Harald Paetz, c. 1870; C.c.; DKKk.
417. Harald Paetz, c. 1870; C. de v.; DKKk.
418. Georg Lindström, 1901; C.c. (14.9 × 8 cm); E. Beck collection.
419. Harald Paetz, c. 1870; C. de v.; DKKt.
420. Georg Rosenkilde, c. 1871; C. de v.; DKKt.
421. Georg Rosenkilde, c. 1871; C. de v.; DKKt.
422. Harald Paetz, c. 1872; C. de v.; DKKk.
423. Harald Paetz, c. 1872; C. de v.; DKKt. Note how Westberg in this photograph supports her *own* head, thus imitating a situation in the fifth scene of Act IV, where Sigyn, while supporting Loke's head, catches the dripping venom from the poisonous snake.
424. Unknown photographer, taken for the production March 8, 1905; photograph (12.7 × 17.2 cm) mounted in album signed 'Ulrik Valentiner 1936'; DKKkt. Scenery originally painted by Valdemar Gyllich (1871). Remounted by Gyllich (1874) with only minor alterations from his own previous set in order to fit the dimensions of the new theatre. In use until 1923. A comparison between this photograph and Gyllich's sketch for the original 1871 décor (reproduced in Svend Kragh-Jacobsen and Torben Krogh, *Den Kongelige Danske Ballet*, between pp. 288 and 289) serves as a fine example of how little the sceneries were changed in their general structure as well as in details. This set was almost completely unchanged from 1871 to 1923 — which is also true for many of the other sceneries presented in this book. The reason for this rather conservative holding on to the original décors in Bournonville's ballets can be explained as a strange mixture of economics and true veneration for the ballets' scenic traditions.
425. N. C. Hansen, O. C. R. Schou, and F. C. L. Weller, c. 1890; C.c.; DKKt.
426. Peter Elfelt, October 1907; neg. (plate no. 4867); DKKk. This photograph is number 8 in an exceptionally long series of twenty-three pictures with Hans Beck performing the rôle of Edouard. The series (Elfelt neg. plates nos. 4860–4882) testifies to the enormous popularity Hans Beck achieved in this particular ballet.
427. Harald Paetz, c. 1871; C. de v.; DKKt.
428. Peter Elfelt, April 17, 1905; neg. (plate no. 3715); DKKk. Note the wig worn by Richard Jensen — a custom quite widespread among male dancers in the 1890s and the first two decades of this century.
429. Peter Elfelt, taken between February 1899 and April 1900; unmounted photograph (14 × 10.4 cm); E. Freddie collection.
430. N. C. Hansen and F. C. L. Weller, taken between 1877 and 1885; C. de v.; DKKk. As this is really a portrait, Frederikke Madsen has here been photographed *without* the mask she actually wears during the performance of the *Polka Militaire*.
431. Peter Elfelt, March 1912; neg. (plate no. 6869); DKKk. Note the cap, which indicates that Merrild here is depicted in the *Polka Militaire*, since the four Volunteers (Steffen, Otto, Carl, and Edouard) changed their helmets for these smaller caps when performing the polka.
432. Peter Elfelt, May 3, 1905; neg. (plate no. 3746); DKKk.
433. Peter Elfelt, May 3, 1905; C.c. (plate no. 3748); DKKt. In the original 1871 production the *Pas de trois* was performed by Emil, Else, and Trine. Since the production on March 8, 1905, however, the *Pas de trois* has been performed by Dirck (or Otto) together with Sophie and Andrea. The costume shown here was later also used in Marius Petipa's *Les Millions d'Harlequin* (premiered on December 9, 1906 with new choreography devised

by Emilie Walbom).

434. Emil Hohlenberg, taken between March 1889 and November 22, 1890; C.c.; DKKt. In the original 1871 production the Reel was performed by Jan, Dirck and an unnamed Volunteer, together with Else, Trine and two unnamed Amager girls. Since the 1905 production, however, the Reel has been performed by Edouard, Jan, Dirck, Else, Trine, and two unnamed Amager girls. The reason for having Edouard taking part in the Reel may well be because of Hans Beck, who performed in it as Emil in 1889 and instantly made it one of his most popular rôles ever. In the 1905 production he took over the rôle of Edouard, and from then on Edouard has always been the centre figure in this lively dance. A film (28 metres) of the Reel was shot by Peter Elfelt in 1906 in his studio in Østergade 24. It shows Hans Beck, Valborg Guldbrandsen, and Ellen Price de Plane performing a shortened version of the dance. From this rare film a glimpse of Hans Beck's true mastery can be obtained (Elfelt moving picture negative no. 129).
435. Peter Newland, May 1918; unmounted photograph (17 × 22.8 cm); E. Merrild collection. Showcase photograph taken in the dance studio of the Royal Theatre for a summer tour in Denmark arranged and headed by Karl Merrild, 1918. For this tour the Reel was extended to be performed by four couples instead of the original cast of three men and four women.
436. Emil Hohlenberg, c. October 1876; C. de v.; DKKt.
437. Heinrich Diedrich, Autumn 1875; C. de v.; DKKt.
438. Harald Paetz, taken between May 1875 and February 1876; C. de v.; DKKt.
439. Harald Paetz, taken between May 1875 and February 1876; C. de v.; DKKk.
440. N. C. Hansen and F. C. L. Weller, taken between May 1875 and February 1876; C.c.; DKKk.
441. Peter Elfelt, December 14, 1904; neg. (plate no. 3585); DKKk.
442. Peter Elfelt, December 14, 1904; neg. (plate no. 3586); DKKk.
443. Peter Most, c. 1876; C. de v.; DKKt.
444. Peter Elfelt, December 14, 1904; neg. (plate no. 3581); DKKt. A film of this dance (29 metres) was shot by Elfelt in 1905 with the two same dancers shown here (Elfelt moving picture neg. no. 110). Note the jockey's fashion of placing their horsewhips in the legs of their boot.
445. Peter Elfelt, December 14, 1904; neg. (plate no. 3582); DKKt.
446. Peter Elfelt, December 14, 1904; neg. (plate no. 3578); DKKt.
447. Peter Elfelt, December 14, 1904; neg. (plate no. 3579); DKKt.
448. Peter Most c. 1876; C.c.; DKKk.
449. Thor Larsen, April 1919; unmounted photograph (23.8 × 16.8 cm) DKKkt.
450. E. Lange, c. 1855/56; C. de v.; K. A. Jürgensen collection.
451. Emil Hohlenberg, c. 1883 C. de v.; DKKt.
452. Peter Elfelt, February 1908; neg. (plate no. 5061); DKKk. Showcase photograph taken for a charity performance at Nørrebro Teater (Copenhagen), February 1908.
453. Peter Elfelt, February 1908; neg. (plate no. 5063); DKKk. See note for no. 452.
454. Thor Larsen, April 1919; unmounted photograph (17.1 × 20.3 cm); DKKkt. Showcase photograph taken for a charity performance at the Casino Theatre (Copenhagen) on April 4, 1919, to celebrate the forthcoming reunification of southern Jutland with the Kingdom of Denmark (see also note for no. 406).
455. Sofus Peter Christensen and E. L. & L. J. Morange, taken between 1885 and 1888; C.c.; DKKk.
456. Sophus Juncker-Jensen, 1906; C.c.; M. Castenskiold collection. *Pas des Trois Cousines* was rehearsed in August and September, 1905, as part of the preparations for the centennial birthday performance in Bournonville's honour, given on August 31, 1905. It was, however, not included in the actual performance, but only practised at the school. This Cabinet card is dated with the inscription: 'Pas des trois Cousines, Januar 1906'.
457. Theodor Collin, c. 1861/62 (outdoor shot); C. de v.; DKKt.
458. Georg Rosenkilde, taken between September 1868 and autumn 1871; C. de v.; DKKt.
459. Harald Paetz, September 9, 1870; C. de v.; DKKt.
460. Same as no. 459.
461. Same as no. 458.
462. Harald Paetz, taken between October 1871 and June 1873; C. de v.; DKKk.
463. Same as no. 462.
464. Unknown photographer, taken for the production October 5, 1913; photograph (11.4 × 16.9 cm) mounted in *Scenebilledalbum (grå)*, p. 125; DKKkt. Scenery originally by Arnold Wallich (1830) freely adapted from Pierre-Luc-Charles Ciceri's original décor at the Paris Opéra (premiered on February 29, 1828), which represented a life-like picture of Naples's Piazza del mercato, with the church and bell-tower of Santa Croce and a great number of street shops. Rearranged set by Troels Lund (1847) with only minor alterations from

Wallich's set. Completely new scenery arranged by Valdemar Gyllich (1875) with partial use of older sets and props from *Napoli* in order to fit the dimensions of the new theatre, and representing a life-like picture of Naples' Largo fuori Porta Capuana. Remounted with only minor alterations from Gyllich's set by Thorolf Pederson for the production on October 5, 1913 (seen here). In use until September 15, 1915, when the opera was given its last performance. The famous Porta Capuana in Naples, erected by Giuliano da Majano in 1485, served as model for Gyllichs's 1875 set. Behind the right tower can be seen the cupola of Santa Caterina a Formiello.

465. Georg Rosenkilde, 1864; C. de v.; DKKk.
466. Same as no. 465.
467. Unknown photographer, taken for the production October 5, 1913; photograph (11.4 × 16.9 cm) mounted in *Scenebilledalbum (grå)*, p. 125; DKKkt.
In the original 1830 production Act IV had scenery by Arnold Wallich representing: 'Portici. The interior of Masaniello's cottage with a door to an adjoining room. In the background, an exit closed with an old ship's sail. At front stage to the right, a table and a chair; to the left, a couch made of straw.' (*Det kongelige Theatres Repertoire, nr. 26*, p. 8). This rather poor scenery was a great disappointment to the Danish audience, who had looked forward especially to seeing the spectacular view of Naples burning in the far distance at the moment in Act IV when Fenella drew aside the sail in the background, as was the case in Pierre-Luc-Charles Ciceri's original décor at the Paris Opéra. In the first production at the new Royal Theatre on October 3, 1875, therefore, the set of Act IV was replaced by the set of Act II (also originally painted by Arnold Wallich), which for this production had been repainted by Valdemar Gyllich with partial use of the older sets in order to fit the dimensions of the new theatre. This set was remounted with only minor alterations by Thorolf Pedersen for the last production of the opera on October 5, 1913 (seen here). In use until September 15, 1915 when the opera was given its last performance.

468. N. C. Hansen, O. C. R. Schou and F. C. L. Weller; taken between 1869 and 1877; C.c.; DKKk.
469. Harald Paetz, 1886; C.c.; DKKt.
470. Holger Damgaard, taken for the production October 5, 1913; unmounted photograph (11.7 × 17.4 cm); DKKk.
471. Georg Rosenkilde, 1864; C. de v.; DKKt.
472. Unknown photographer, taken for the production March 12, 1915 or earlier (1902?); photograph (12 × 17 cm) mounted in *Maskinmesterprotokol, Mappe 18, nr. 2* (1915–16); DKKkt.
Scenery originally painted by C. F. Christensen (1865). New scenery arranged by Valdemar Gyllich (1878) with partial use of older sets in order to fit the dimensions of the new theatre. Remounted by Thorolf Pedersen for the production on November 1, 1899 (seen here) with only minor alterations from Gyllich's previous set. In use until December 4, 1917.
473. Peter Most, c. 1876; C. de v.; DKKt.
474. Harald Paetz, c. May 1885; C. de v.; DKKt.
475. Peter Elfelt, May 23, 1906; neg. (plate no. 4205); DKKk.
This photograph is an enlargement of a frame from a film (36 metres) shot by Elfelt in his studio in Østergade 24 on May 23, 1906 (Elfelt moving picture neg. no. 139).
476. Peter Elfelt, March 13, 1919; neg. (plate no. 7053); DKKk.
477. Unknown photographer, taken for the production November 1, 1921; photograph (11 × 16.6 cm) mounted in *Maskinmesterprotokol 29, serie 1* (1921–22); DKKkt.
Scenery originally by C. F. Christensen (1842). New scenery arranged by Valdemar Gyllich, 1873, and again with minor alterations in 1875 with partial use of the older sets in order to fit the dimensions of the new theatre. Completely new scenery painted by Thorolf Pedersen for the opera's last production on November 1, 1921 (seen here). In use until December 10, 1921 when the opera was given its last performance.
478. Peter Most, c. 1875; C. de v.; DKKt.

Bibliography

BOOKS AND PERIODICALS WITH LARGE NUMBERS OF PHOTOGRAPHS OF
BOURNONVILLE'S BALLETS

Agerholm, Edvard, *Den Danske Ballet 1870–1915* (Copenhagen, Erslev & Hasselbalch, 1915).

Cavling, Viggo, *Ballettens Bog* (Copenhagen, Alfred G. Hassings Forlag, 1941).

Reumert, Elith, *Den Danske Ballets Historie* (Copenhagen, Hjemmets Forlag, 1922).

Hver 8. Dag, no. 13 (December 25, 1904, Copenhagen, G. Kalckar).

Teatret (Copenhagen, Jens Petersen and Albert Gnudtzmann, m. fl., 1901–31).

OTHER GENERAL WORKS ON BOURNONVILLE AND/OR OF ICONOGRAPHIC
INTEREST

Aschengreen, Erik, *Balletbogen* (Copenhagen, Gyldendal, 1982).

Aschengreen, Erik (and others), *Perspektiv på Bournonville* (Copenhagen, Nyt Nordisk Forlag Arnold Busck, 1980).

Bech, Viben and Andersen, Ellen, *Kostumer og modedragter fra Det kgl. Teaters herregarderobe* (Copenhagen, Nationalmuseet, 1979).

Fridericia, Allan, *August Bournonville* (Copenhagen, Rhodos, 1979).

Kragh-Jacobsen, Svend and Krogh, Torben, *Den Kongelige Danske Ballet* (Copenhagen, Selskabet til udgivelse af kulturskrifter, 1952).

Westrup, August and Bojesen, Ernst, *Minder fra Teaterverdenen* (Copenhagen, Ernst Bojesens Kunstforlag, 1881–83).

ADDITIONAL SOURCES

Anonymous: *Reqvisit = Bog No. 1* (Stage director's handwritten list of props, 1829–42); Collection of Karen Krogh, Copenhagen.

Anonymous: *Reqvisit = Bog No. 2* (Stage director's handwritten list of props) *Begÿndt d: 16.de Junii 1843*; Collection of Karen Krogh, Copenhagen.

Anonymous: *Scenemesterbøger 1–12* (Stage director's records 1–12, 1835–67); Collection of Karen Krogh, Copenhagen.

Anonymous: *Bog 559, Decorationer, Meubler m:v: Det kongelige Theater tilhörende* (July 1866 – November 19, 1872) Det kgl. Teaters Arkiv L, Rigsarkivet (State Archive), Copenhagen.

Anonymous: *Bog 560, Decorationer etc. 1874*, Det kgl. Teaters Arkiv L, Rigsarkivet (State Archive), Copenhagen.

Aumont, Arthur and Collin, Edgar, *Det danske Nationaltheater 1748–1889 En Statistisk Fremstilling II*, (Copenhagen, Alfred G. Hassings Forlag, 1899).

Bech, Peter, *Billedregistrant til Tidsskriftet 'Teatret' (1901–31)* (Privately printed, 1977).

Bournonville, August, *My Theatre Life*, translated from the Danish by Patricia N. McAndrew, (Middletown, Conn., Wesleyan University Press, 1979).

Bournonville, August, 'The Ballet Poems by August Bournonville: The Complete Scenarios', translated from the Danish by Patricia N. McAndrew, *Dance Chronicle*, Vol. 3, No. 2 – Vol. 6. No. 1, (New York, Marcel Dekker, 1979–83).

Elfelt, Peter, *Protokoller* (handwritten ledgers):
a) *Kabinet* (Cabinet card photos), 4 volumes: 1898–1905, 1906–1909, 1910–1912, 1913–1916;
b) *Skiltebilleder*, (Showcase photos), 2 volumes: 1890–1904, 1905–1913; Copenhagen: Royal Library, Picture Department.

Elfelt, Peter, *Fortegnelse over Levende Billeder optaget mellem 1899–1920* (handwritten Catalogue of Moving Pictures shot between 1899 and 1920), Copenhagen, Royal Library, Picture Department.
Note: The Elfelt films (with a sound track of the original music added in 1978 by pianist Elvi Henriksen) include dances from *La Sylphide* (1903), *Napoli* (1903), *From Siberia to Moscow* (1905), *The King's Corps of Volunteers on Amager* (1906), *The Troubadour* (1906), and *La Sylphide* (1906).
The films are today preserved in *Danmarks Radio* (Danish Television) and Dance Film Archive, University of Rochester, Rochester, N.Y. 14627, U.S.A.

Guest, Ivor, *Adeline Genée* (London, Adam and Charles Black, 1958).

Guest, Ivor, *Fanny Cerrito* (London, Dance Books Ltd., 1974).

Guest, Ivor, *The Ballet of the Second Empire 1858–1870 & 1847–1858* (2 volumes, London, Adam and Charles Black, 1953 & 1955).

Guest, Ivor, *The Romantic Ballet in Paris*, 2nd revised edition (London, Dance Books Ltd, 1980).

Hallar, Marianne and Leicht, Georg, *Det kongelige Teaters Repertoire 1889–1975* (Odense, Bibliotekscentralens Forlag, 1977).

Hallar, Marianne, 'August Bournonville's balletter 1877–1977' in Aschengreen, Erik, *Ballettens Digter: 3 Bournonville essays* (Copenhagen, Rhodos, 1977).

Hansen, Peter, *Den danske Skueplads II–III* (Copenhagen, Ernst Bojesens Kunstforlag, 1881–93).

Kempe, Fritz, *Daguerreotypie in Deutschland* (Seebruck am Chiemsee, Heering Verlag, 1979).

Mørk, Ebbe (and others), *Salut for Bournonville* (Copenhagen, Statens Museum for Kunst, 1979).

Neiiendam, Robert, *Det kongelige Teaters Historie I* (Copenhagen, Branner, 1921).

Ochsner, Bjørn, *Fotografer i og fra Danmark til og med år 1920* (Photographers in and from Denmark up to and including 1920: Odense, Bibliotekscentralens Forlag, 1986).

Theatre Research Studies II (Copenhagen, The Institute for Theatre Research, 1972).

Indexes

In the following, page numbers are given in roman: numbers in italic refer to photographs and/or notes to be found in the List of Pictures (p. 163).

INDEX A

Dancers, Actors and Singers in mime rôles, Choreographers, Ballet Masters

INDEX B
Composers, Costumiers, Scene Painters

INDEX C

Writers, Painters, Sculptors and others

INDEX D

Photographers

INDEX E
Ballets, Operas, Plays, Divertissements and Single Dances

179